KEEPING IT SIMPLE

Sorting Out
What Really Matters in Your Life

Gary S. Aumiller, Ph.D.

PRESS
750 VETERANS MEMORIAL HIGHWAY
HAUPPAUGE, NEW YORK 11788

To My Family
Roy, Linda, Lisa and Tony Aumiller

Acknowledgements

Thanks to: Dennis Fico, Pat Moran, Newell and Terry Brown, Ed and Sue Fox, Jeff Levine, Petronela Perlz, Doug Darrell, Sonny Fragala, Steve and Demetria Ehlman, Dennis and Jill Conley, Barry and Sharon Parker, Wendy Silverman and Robert and Anne Ramsey for their encouragement and for showing me the simple pleasures of friendship.

Thanks to: Mihael Mahoney, Tomn Tohill, Jeff Frayler, Pete O'Leary and the boards of the Suffolk County PBA, Detectives Association and Correction Officers Assocation for their assistaence with my career which allows me the honor of helping law enforcement officers and their families.

Special Thanks to: Dr. Daniel and Lisa Goldfarb, Rebecca Anderson and Father Joe D'Angelo for their suggestion and proofreading throughout this project. Also thanks to my agent Nancy Yost for her patience in working with my writing and ideas.

And finally, thanks to Sally Walsh who taught me to enjoy writing.

Published by Probity Press
750 Veterans Memorial Highway, Hauppauge, NY 11788

ISBN 0-9667454-C-X
(previously published by Adams Publishing, ISBN 1-55850-498-2)
Printed in the United States
Second Edition 1998
First Edition 1995

Aumiller, Gary, S.
   Keeping it simple: sorting out what really matters in your life/
Gary S. Aumiller. --
   ISBN 0-9667454-C-X
   1. Simplicity.   2. Stress (Psychology) -- Prevention I. Title
   BJ1496.A95   1995

This book is available at quantity discounts for bulk purchases.
For information call 516-724-5522

TABLE OF CONTENTS

PROLOGUE

A Simple Piece of Ice

I sat and dutifully listened to a story I had heard many times from my parents and now from my friend's Brooklyn relatives. It seems that people who were children of the forties and before remember a time when there was no refrigeration in their homes. To compensate for what seems a necessity nowadays, people had ice blocks delivered to their homes from a centralized ice house. These blocks were put in an ice box with all the perishables that needed to be kept cool. This process led to one of the world's simplest pleasures, and a pleasure that I have envied since the first time I heard this story.

As the ice man would travel down the street on a hot summer day, a pack of children followed his truck. As he chipped off a hunk of ice from the big block to fill each order, small pieces would break off. These small pieces of ice were given to the children to cool themselves down in the summer heat. Each small piece of ice was cherished, bringing immeasurable pleasure to the overheated children—who are now misty-eyed adults remembering the gleeful event fifty years later. Imagine, a piece of ice—frozen water. Is there anything simpler?

Today, when ice cream comes in thousands of flavors, with exotic names like double-fudge-upside-down-magic-cookie-and-cream-monster crunch, I would still bet that those simple pieces of ice brought more pleasure to those kids. In fact, I would be willing to venture that most of us will never know a pleasure comparable to that simple "piece of ice." It is sad to realize that in a time so filled with the "riches" of life—modern conveniences, inventions, and gadgets—that we actually live in great poverty for the pleasure of simple things, like that little piece of ice.

In an attempt to make life easier, we make life more complicated. In an attempt to better meet our perceived needs, we deny our basic needs. In an attempt to create some sense of lasting happiness, we set the conditions for happiness to be transient. By doing so, we are messing up. Happiness was around long before we intervened. Happiness was, and still is, related to focusing on simple pleasures.

Sports cars, VCRs, CDs, Nintendos, wide-screen TVs, 100-watts-per-channel stereos, automatic ice makers, microwaves, cellular phones, automatic garage door openers, automatic tellers, Jacuzzis, psychoanalysis, self-analysis, home computers, exercise cycles, belly crunch machines, adjustable vibrating beds, and remote control living rooms are all examples of *more*. The devices and toys that we have adorned ourselves with in the past two decades to entertain, amuse, make life more convenient, or attempt to make ourselves happier are truly amazing. Children of the seventies, eighties, and now the nineties will experience or have already experienced "things" that could not even have been imagined by children of previous decades. Yet, although these generations will have all this and *more*, I believe that they will be the poorest of generations when it comes to appreciating real pleasures. *More* will add up to *more* stress, *more* broken relationships, *more* distance from one's own spirit.

Why would we choose to deny ourselves pleasure? In reality the choice is made in ignorance. After all, we are motivated to increase pleasure and decrease pain. Freud and his followers have called this the pleasure principle. However, we have been suckered into believing that the source of pleasure is not in the development of what we already have but in the acquisition of *more*. Sometimes *more* means less!

How can more mean less? When the possession of *more* costs a disproportionate amount in life's complications than it produces in life's pleasures. When you spend a disproportionate amount of time earning and maintaining the "things" of *more* than spent enjoying those "things." When you spend *more* time examining the complexities of your life than enjoying the activities of your life. When spirituality adds *more* hassles to your life and seems to miss the real meaning. When *more* separates you from the people you love rather than bringing you together. When you spend *more* time thinking how to feel good than you do feeling good. When, if given a piece of ice, you complain about the lack of flavor, or that another person has a larger piece of ice.

Do you really believe that people in our society are happier than the settlers on the Western frontier who had very little? Are our children today happier playing Nintendo than the children of the thirties following the ice truck? We have been made to believe that technology will provide the hope for mankind. We've been made to believe that a psychological understanding of our inner selves will transform us. The hope for mankind does not lie in scientific advances that add to *more*. It does not lie in the creation of bigger and better toys. But happiness does not lie in any complex techniques of psychology designed to give you new insights into the inner self. The hope for mankind lies in the focus on the "simple things" in life. The hope for mankind may actually be a step back in a time when science is propelling the world forward at a phenomenal pace.

So you say, "I like my *more*. I don't want to do without." Please don't mistake this book as a prescription to move into a homemade cabin on the shores of Walden Pond (although this may be the answer for some). You will *not* be told to strip yourself of your possessions that you've spent your life working toward. You *will* be asked to search your personal philosophy of life and focus on the "simple ideas" that are more effective in guiding your life. You *will* be asked to look at the sources of pleasure and recognize the lasting quality of the "simple pleasures." And, you *will* be asked to look at your possessions and evaluate the "simple things" that are important to happiness. *This book will teach you how to fight the trend toward complication and make your life more simple and thus happier. Simplification, not complication.*

It's time for a new discipline in psychology to help people learn to reduce the complexity of their lives until they are happy. Reduction makes life simpler, adding makes life more complicated. The simpler life is a happier life.

I have worked for ten years with police and corrections officers. Every day they face risking their lives. They must work within institutional rules, work in rotating schedules, and live a work life where they see only the bad parts of the world. The stress the job places on them is tremendous and, unfortunately, gets expressed in high divorce rates, high rates of alcoholism, unbelievable rates of job burnout, and high suicide rates. I found that traditional methods of psychotherapy did not work with these officers—they needed something other than the couch.

It was obvious that these officers' lives were overstressed, overtaxed and overcomplicated. They were unnecessarily analyzing every event in their lives. They were overstretching their budgets at home, overtaxing their work schedules to pay for extravagance. They took their relationships for granted and did not work to maintain healthy connections with people. They seemed to have lost their identities, subordinating their sense of self to the roles they played in life. They had lost all sense of spirituality. They had become too complicated to feel alive.

We began working on simplifying their lives. The response was tremendous. They felt better. They looked better. They enjoyed the people and events in their lives that they had overlooked. They found new pursuits that were pleasure-rich. They became alive again—simpler yet more alive. If these techniques can work with the most stressed-out of law enforcement populations, they can make a tremendous change in the lives of people who do not face such intense daily threats and stresses.

This book demonstrates the process of "keeping it simple" by following the path of one police officer, Mike, who came to psychotherapy as many people do—afraid, with his life in a shambles from complications. The officer is a "composite" of many police patients. The therapist is also a composite, perhaps more similar to his patient than many people want to believe. The book follows these two characters through twenty-one sessions of therapy designed to help Mike simplify and sort out what is really important in his life. The dialogue style of this book was chosen to make it easier for you to learn from Mike's experience, and to better apply the principles to your own life. It should both enhance your capacity to identify with the process and the course of his change. The dialogue format is especially appropriate to this book because it forces ideas to be expressed more simply, and simpler is better.

Each of us has a "piece of ice" in our memory and in our present life. However, most of us seem to ignore the ice truck even when it is on the street in front of our house. We focus on what we think are bigger and better pleasures that end up costing us by complicating our lives. Once complicated, we begin to focus on simply maintaining the status quo, which further complicates our lives. The result is a whole destructive circle of complications. The process continues until we find ourselves burned out, over-stressed, ready to explode. We can face our complications by just trying to stop long enough to relax, or by focusing on what we are really missing.

If you have found yourself stressed out or desperately "needing a vacation," then you are losing sight of the simple life. If you have found yourself losing patience with people or frustrated that nobody seems to be doing what they should, then you are losing sight of the simple life. If you find that you spend an inordinate amount of your time worrying or being unhappy, then you will read about yourself again and again in these pages. When you learn the process of *Keeping It Simple*, you will be able to recapture the sweet "taste of ice" in your life.

SESSION 1

The Heavy Badge

Mike is a man's man. The type who, when he shakes your hand, you know he's been there. He looks you straight in the eye, talking with the gruffness of coarse-grained sandpaper. He is about 6'4", 44 years old, with blond hair and a powerful build. His forearms are painted with perfectly-placed hair and long, deep cuts of muscle. He played football at a medium-sized college in the Midwest, then went into the marines where, in short order, he became a sergeant. Mike has one of those sharply cut faces that appears unshaven even minutes after a razor. He is like a big brown bear—soft and easy-going in some respects, but severe and imposing in others. He so personifies the image of a cop that his picture was once used on a poster showing him in uniform wearing one of those big round-brimmed hats. The slogan read "Don't Drink and Drive" as Mike shut the prison door on an inebriated motorist.

When he walked into my office there was a different image. His voice was strained as he tried to make casual conversation.

"Getting warm. Full moon tonight. Guess all the nuts will be coming out, huh, Doc?"

Cops have a way of letting you know what role they want you to play.

"I don't work with nuts, Mike, I work with cops. Do cops come out with the full moon, too?"

A psychologist for cops has to define his own place.

"If you work with us, you must be a busy guy."
"Too busy for small talk. You see the Giants game yesterday, Mike?"

In therapy, you have to sneak up on a cop.

"Yeah, some game. Thought they'd pull it out."
"Glad they lost. I'm a Redskins fan. Grew up in Maryland. So, why are you here?"

I've heard people say that cops don't express feelings well. I'm not sure that's true. I do know they never seem to talk in full sentences. They also like to "bullshit" a lot, but if you talk "bull" with them too long, you'll never get anywhere.

"Redskins, huh. I used to ..." (cut off)
"So, why are you here?"
"It's all messed up, Doc. I need help. I need to get out of this mess."
"Had sort of a rough time lately, Mike?"
"Look, I'm not used to talking about myself. I'm not sure I can do this."
"Are you on the street, Mike?"

Time to set a trap.

"Yeah."
"Now, let me get this right. You can go into a domestic dispute, not knowing whether someone is going to pull a gun out and shoot your ass, but you're too threatened to sit in front of some half-awake beard-ed guy with letters behind his name and tell him whether you wear boxer or jockey shorts. It doesn't make much sense, Mike."

Mike quietly chuckled a little, picked the inside of his right eyetooth with his left index finger and started to talk.

"I don't know where it started, but it sure is a mess now. I feel like shit every day. All I ever do with my wife is argue. All I ever do is yell at the kids. They don't even care about me anymore. There's so much tension at home it feels like I'm swimming in Jell-O. I have a girlfriend, who was a good release for awhile, but now she's pressuring me because I should have left my wife by now. I know it's wrong, but I need her, Doc, just to get away from the rest of the crap. It seems everywhere I go, I get shit. I'd like to just run away and forget it all. Start over. What should I do?"

I'm convinced that if I was able to run off two or three suggestions right now, Mike would go away happy. He wouldn't have to talk anymore, wouldn't have to change, and whatever happened next in his life, he could say he tried psychotherapy and it didn't work.

"Your life sounds complicated as hell, Mike. How long have you been on the job?"

"Eighteen years."

"How long married?"

"Eight years."

"How long was your first marriage?"

Deep sigh. Look away. Mike looked like a dog who just wet on the rug and knew the rolled paper was coming.

"Seven years. I was too young to be married the first time. Started dating my present wife and got a divorce. Guess all cops have one or two ex's."

"Sounds like you did try to start over once, Mike. How old are the kids?"

"Well, I have two boys from this marriage. Michael is seven and Kenny is five. My daughter is a sophomore in college. She's eighteen or nineteen, I guess."

"Do you and your daughter get along?"

"We didn't when I was living there, but after I moved out, our relationship got better. Now, I've sort of lost touch with her, except a college bill every semester. She is always angry at me for some reason or another. Just like her mother."

"What does your wife think the problem is with your marriage now?"

"She says I should spend more time with the family. I should show her I love her. I shouldn't always be in a bad mood. I think she shouldn't overreact to everything. She's crazy all the time now."

"Are you spending enough time at home? I mean, you've got the job and the girlfriend and everything."

"The girlfriend came later. I always looked at the other cops with their mistresses when I was young and thought I'd never cheat. But now here I am. Anyway, I work a lot. It's hard to afford a family, pay child support, college tuition, and everything else. I mean, kids need a lot of things. They don't just want a ten dollar pair of sneakers anymore. They need $150 'Air this or that.' I'm always writing checks. Christmas cost me over a thousand dollars last year. Then, my wife needs to have things too. She buys so much the house gets cluttered. Credit card bills mount up. All that damn interest. Some of them charge 21 percent interest! We moved to a good neighborhood so the kids will have better schools. My wife doesn't understand that I work extra time so the family can have all the things they need. She should understand. She just yells about how I'm not home and how we still don't have the money we need. You can't have both. We've had some vicious arguments. That's when I started to go out with the guys and found Carol, my girlfriend. At least I was happy with her before she started getting on my case all the time. She should leave me alone a little."

"Which 'she' are we talking about?"

"What do you mean?"

"Mike, you said, 'I was happy before she started getting on my case all the time.' Is this the girlfriend 'she' or the wife 'she' that is getting on your case?"

Mike starts that little quiet chuckle and tooth picking again.

"Why do I feel like you're playing with my head?"

"Sorry, Mike. I guess that comes from my high school jock days. You know, you see something that looks like a basketball, ya gotta dribble it a little."

Mike laughed out loud this time. Then he stated, proudly,

"I guess you're suggesting that I set myself up for both these women to get on my case?"

"Don't be too happy with yourself, Mike. Insight is just a start. It doesn't necessarily help you change."

"Well, it's not all my fault or my wife's. My wife was abused as a kid. Not physically abused but mentally abused. Her parents still do a lot of things they shouldn't, like put all kinds of guilt on her and tell her she can't do anything right. My life was no parade either. My father was always kicking my butt for one reason or another. He drank all the time. I mean we probably didn't stand a chance from the beginning."

"And let me guess. Your mom was codependent, your dad was a rage-aholic, you lost you inner child, your toilet training was all wrong, and there were so many blue-colored rooms in the house you couldn't help but be depressed all the time."

"What's your point?"

✦ "I guess I just don't like when we concoct 'special ways' to say people have problems. It's like making up arbitrary excuses for unhealthy actions. It doesn't change what you have to do to get better."

"Yeah, but after years of people cutting you down, it all builds up. It's easier to say I'm gonna change than do it."

"Mike, you don't fall on the top of a mountain—you climb there. Mental health is like physical health. You work at it every day to get into shape and to stay in shape. The more out of shape you are when you start, the longer you have to work and the more sore you feel after the workouts. You can't get into mental shape unless you work hard at it."•

Silence. They call it "therapeutic silence" in psychotherapy textbooks. It is supposed to be a time when the client processes what is said. Gets insight. A good therapist is supposed to allow silence to occur even though it is very uncomfortable for both shrink and patient. I have a problem with silence. I can't see being paid up to two dollars a minute, 90 to a 100 dollars a fifty-minute hour, to remain silent and make someone uncomfortable. I always break silence quickly.

"So, how do you like the new guns they gave you guys?"

"They're pretty good. Much better than the old .38's. More comforting. It's nice to know you've got seventeen rounds of hydra-shock, hollow point, nine millimeter at your side in a gunfight rather than just six 'FBI load' .38's."

"I haven't shot the new guns. The plastic bothers me a little. Makes it look like a toy. So, Mike, what's the job like?"

"Ah, Doc, they never leave you alone either. I wish they'd just let me do my job and leave me alone. Although, I have to admit, sometimes I'd rather be at the job than at home, or anywhere else for that matter. At least I get to relax between calls."

"How has the job changed since you came on?"

"It used to be a lot of fun. You know, being with the guys and all. I used to be 'Super Cop.' I figured if I worked extra hard I'd 'get made' detective in no time. I wrote a lot of summonses. I made a lot of arrests. I helped everybody I could who was in trouble. But, it seems in order to 'be made' you gotta know somebody. It's all political. I'm not going to play politics to get a promotion I deserve. So I got overlooked every time. You know, I was doing a walking tour for awhile. So, I figured I'd write a summons an hour. A fair number. I get called in and told that I'm making the other guys look bad. I should go to the movies like everyone else and if they need me they'll call. It shouldn't be that way. It's stupid. Not fair."

"When did you finally decide to stop trying to make detective?"

"A few years ago when they tried to 'do me.' I stop this drunk driving a car when I'm on midnights. He resists. I cuff him. Turns out he's a lawyer. He charges me with brutality because he knows that it will take the focus off his DWI. Internal affairs gets involved and they treat me like I'm the criminal—guilty until proven innocent. Like I pulled over this poor innocent motorist and beat him up for fun. People forget that I'm just a regular guy trying to do a job. They don't picture me sitting in front of the TV with my little son. All of a sudden, I'm the bad guy. Eventually, it all got dropped. The charges, the DWI, my morale. I gave up at that point. Now I'm just biding time until I can retire."

"You've really had it all go downhill for you at once."

"I can't believe this is me. I used to be the life of the party. I used to go to church every Sunday. I used to be a decent guy."

"What happened to church?"

"Well, that's another story. I guess that got complicated too. You know, you've got to agree with them on other issues than just God, like abortion, birth control, capital punishment ... I guess I just can't agree with them, so I stopped going. I miss it. I feel like I don't belong to anything anymore."

"You're lost. Without direction. Trying ..."

Mike cuts me off: "Trying to salvage a little bit of happiness each day. That's it. I live moment to moment, trying to find even a second of happiness to smile about. I've got no future, just a clouded picture of today. I can't believe this is me."

"For a guy who thought he'd have trouble talking, you did great. Mike, your life has gotten really complicated. You've lost yourself under the clutter. I can help you, but I can't change your life for you. I'm only a guide, like a dispatcher. I can tell you the direction, but you have to do the work yourself. It's important that you work all the way through from beginning to end and don't stop just because you feel a little better. You've got to hold on to the way you feel now to motivate you, to completely change, so you can fully enjoy life again."

Mike nervously played with an old headband he was wearing that seemed out of place with the rest of his outfit.

"Mike, just out of curiosity, what's with the headband?"

"Well, this is sort of stupid. It's like a superstition I've had since I was in the academy. It's sort of a reminder to keep my head together when the pressure's on. I always wear it on the job, but lately I wear it all the time. It's become like a security blanket, I guess."

"A security blanket to keep you from losing it. Interesting idea. Does it work?"

"I guess not or I wouldn't be here. Who knows, maybe it worked for awhile. When do we get started? I'm ready to work, Doc. What do I do?"

"Before we start, Mike, there's something you're not telling me. I can sense it. I want to know what that is, Mike."

I call this "the question." I couldn't sense anything, really. This is one of those psychologist's tricks to get that last bit of information out of people. It makes him think I can read his mind or something. When I did my training for my doctorate degree, I used to save "the question" until after a few sessions. I asked "the question" after eight sessions the very first time I worked with a cop. We had been working on family problems and the like, and I asked "the question" figuring I'd get some inconsequential bit of information. Instead he tells me he wears women's lingerie under his uniform. I told him I didn't believe him. He dropped his pants and pulled up his shirt to reveal black lace panties and a bra. Imagine being a brand spanking new doctor and your first client is a macho male wearing lace panties, bra, and a .38 caliber handgun. I was completely caught off guard and was slightly nervous about what to say next. I mean, he could have shot me if I reacted wrong. I recognized at that time that working with cops would always pose new challenges. I also realized then that, for my sanity, "the question" should always be asked in the first session.

"Something I'm not telling you. Man, you're good. I've been dealing with this feeling for a long time. But the real reason I decided to come in now was because of a call I went on the other day."

Mike's eye contact shifted; he massaged his forehead and continued.

"The call came through. Gunshot. Unknown origin. We get to this house. Break in and there is this woman who took her husband's shotgun and blew the back of her head off. 12 gauge. It looked like someone shoved a stick of dynamite in her head and it exploded. Brains, hair, all over the place; it was gross. Of course, we joked about it. That's what cops do. They make fun of things to keep their emotions at a distance. But, it really affected me. You don't know how many times I thought about eating my gun. I could have been her. I don't know what's wrong with me. I don't know if you can help me. But Doc, please don't let my head explode."

* * * *

Our world is obsessed with police stories. So many movies and TV shows are about cops or detectives solving crimes, catching criminals, or just running around shooting at somebody for one reason or another. But the shows in our media aren't the real police stories for most cops. Unfortunately, Mike's story is much more common than the shoot-'em-up tales that entertain us so well.

I tell my police officer patients that the longer they wear the badge, the heavier it will get. It gets heavy with complications, heavy with the turmoils that life loads on them. They have a larger cross to bear than most of us because their jobs are complicated by the daily risk they face, from the negative attitudes to work shifts that unsettle family schedules. It takes hard work for them to keep their lives on track, hard work to keep their badges from getting so heavy that they break their backs. The pattern I have observed in police officers, I see in many lives regardless of occupation. Many of us wear a heavy badge.

The average male cops come on the job in their early- to mid-twenties. They are full of life, dripping with confidence. They finish the academy and prepare for lives on the streets with apprenticeships to older, more experienced officers. Socially, they enjoy their youth and the camaraderie of the other young officers. There is always a group for a game of ball, always someone to go out with on the singles scene. There seems to be an abundance of young women; some say they are attracted by the uniform, others feel they are drawn by the confidence. I would suspect female attraction is natural to a group of men who have fun together and have a strong social circle. These young men live in barely furnished apartments or at home with their parents. They have the freedom that can only come from a simple existence. Life is active, full of challenges, and enjoyable.

As higher salaries start coming in, the accumulation of possessions begins—perhaps nicer, sportier cars, nicer furniture, maybe even purchasing places of their own. They travel to fun places on vacation or take trips with the boys for special occasions. They spend their full salaries on daily life and are satisfied.

As they grow older, they start to think about getting more out of life. They start pairing and begin more serious relationships. Some of their activities with the boys are replaced by time with women. Plans are made to begin families. Thoughts change toward stability and marriage.

The first years of marriage form the honeymoon period. The couple is happy together and leads the same kind of active life they did when they were single, except some of the nights with the boys are replaced by couple's nights. In their bliss, they think of children and start forming larger families. His job still offers camaraderie and challenge.

The downside starts somewhere after the family begins to form. Families demand different time commitments, different financial commitments. The officer works on a rotating shift schedule, so he doesn't get to spend the time with his family that is typical of a 9 to 5, Monday through Friday worker. The police wife, due to this schedule, is less likely to work outside the home, or only works part-time. The pressure becomes stronger on the officer to be the "breadwinner." Demands for material "things" increase. Like most fathers, the officer wants his family to have the best "things" possible. So he works harder, often putting in lots of overtime, or even taking a second job. The family buys "things" on credit to increase their possessions or just "make do" between paychecks. The officer's time with the family is greatly diminished. The job begins to be less appealing because it has become too big a part of the officer's life. Their world is out of balance.

Soon the officer starts to feel alienated from his family. He over-identifies his role as a policeman in his life. After all, he is spending more time as a police officer than as a husband and father. The negative part of working with people who break the law starts to wear on the officer and change his thinking about the world. In police psychology, we call the buildup of incidents "accumulated stress." After years of accumulation, frequently an incident happens that becomes the proverbial "straw that breaks the camel's back." He begins to get a negative attitude in many areas of his life. This carries over to his family life.

The negativity starts to strain the relationships between the officer and his wife, and the officer and his children, resulting in more arguments than fun. The officer may further withdraw into his job(s). He may search for the fun life he used to have hanging out with the boys, going back to the single scenes of his youth. He may just stay at home and withdraw in front of the TV set. Usually his actions mean the further demise of his relationships.

The final step in the process is when the officer starts to act in ways that are totally against the moral values he had when he was younger. This can range from having an affair or two, becoming an ogre as a father, or leaving his family and disregarding their needs. His spirit is broken; he functions only to grab moments of pleasure, bit by bit each day, in any way possible, no matter what the cost. Shortly thereafter, the family falls apart. At this point, some officers start over and rebuild, only to repeat the pattern again. Some seek help, and many feel the only option is to take their own life, or "eat their gun" as they call it.

This is Mike's story, a typical police story. It is also the story of many others who don't wear a badge. Mike's life was simple in his youth. Then the demands of the world took over. First was the demand for "things," or possessions. With this came credit card bills and more work to pay for "things." His thoughts started to drift away from his family, his goals fell apart. He lost the significant relationships in his life. Finally, he lost his spirit, his will to live. He fostered destructive impulses.

To overcome the effects of this process, to stimulate a change, Mike must rebuild in the exact order that the deterioration occurred. It's like building a pyramid from the foundation—a Pyramid of Change. At each step Mike must learn to simplify, overcome the complications at that level. The goal at the top is a simpler life.

Perhaps you have watched your life get more complicated. Perhaps you have seen your youth slip away into an overstressed existence. Perhaps your relationships are suffering from these complications. Perhaps you have lost some of your "self" also. You, like Mike, can learn to simplify your life.

As this book demonstrates, you will need to rebuild the pyramid. "Things" form the foundation of the pyramid, then "Thoughts," "Relationships," and finally "Spirituality." This book takes you through Mike's therapy and the reconstruction of his pyramid. If you follow the process with your life, *you* can simplify too.

Each of the four levels is broken into five sessions which will help simplify life. The sessions mirror a psychotherapy session with Mike. In face-to-face psychotherapy, proceeding to the next session is not done until the previous information is completely understood and processed. A summary is provided at the end of each section. Similarly, you may need to review certain sessions to assure your own understanding. Remember, you are building a foundation for a new, more simple life. The stronger the base, the stronger the pyramid.

The exercises at the end of each session are important because they will help you re-program to a more simple life. Wherever possible, I've included Mike's examples and observations. His examples will help you through the exercises and be your guide toward a simpler life.

Complication can destroy you from the ground up, as when a nest of termites attacks your home. Rebuild. Simplify. Be happier. Lighten your "heavy badge."

SESSION 2

Eat, Drink, Urinate, Defecate, and Find Shelter

I never know if a psychotherapy patient will come the second time. For Mike, like other patients, it's actually harder to go the second time than the first. The first meeting the patient is all psyched up, and in the most pain. It's easy because all he has to do is give a little history and get the problem off his chest. By the second meeting, the patient usually feels a little better, so he questions why he is going again. The second meeting is scarier because the work of changing begins. It's actually the first real session.

Mike showed up in his uniform. Badge, gun, and all. He said he had to go to work. If I was one of those analytic therapists, I'd say he did it subconsciously because the uniform gave him power, security, and distance. We'd discuss the uniform as a message to me as the therapist to stay away. I'd worry about the transference or his ability to relate to me while in the uniform. I'd analyze ...

"Nice uniform, Mike. What are you doing, trying to get some free coffee out of me?"

"Nah, I gotta go to work after this session. So here I am. Cure me."

"Cure you! Glad you understood all that stuff about how *you* have to do all the work, and how *you* have to do the mental exercises to get into mental shape."

"Oh yeah, I forgot. Sometimes us cops have heads like a rock."

"A rock, huh? Well that's good, the bullet will just bounce off when you eat your gun."

I like being tough in the first few sessions. It sort of sets the tone for the whole therapy. Joking around can come later.

"Touché. Okay, I'm here, Doc. I'll remember what you say the next time. Now, what do I do?"

"Well, first you listen a lot. I've broken all the issues that we have to change into small, simple lessons. We'll talk about each concept or lesson first, do a couple of exercises, then I'll give you some homework."

"Homework! You've got to be kidding. I was never good at homework. I'm not sure I'll be doing this homework stuff."

"Mike, maybe you ought to go back to the .38 instead of the nine millimeter."

"Why's that?"

" 'Cause the way you're starting this therapy, you may want a .38. It will make a smaller hole in the back of your head."

"Man, why're you making fun of me seeing a woman blow herself away? That was a big event in my life. After all, it got me here, didn't it?"

"In the first place, we don't know whether it's a big event in your life. It's a great story. Very dramatic. I may even use it one day. But it didn't mean diddly if you don't do something while you're here. If it makes you change, then I'll be willing to call it a big event in your life. Secondly, don't tell me you never did homework before. I don't care what you did before. I don't want to know about your mother. I don't want to know about your father. I don't want to hear the story about when you first smoked a cigarette, or got laid. All I care about is what you are going to do now and whether you are going to change or not."

"Understood. But the story about the first time I got laid is a good story."

He was trying to lighten it up a little. I was getting a little rough on him. (Probably shouldn't have had the baked bean special for lunch.)

"Well, maybe you can tell that one after we've finished your therapy and your life is simple again. But for now, follow me closely. Mike, you've been brainwashed!! The people who manufacture and market products in this world have worked on you since your birth. They want you to make false emotional attachments to "things," mere objects. They have brainwashed you to believe the right possessions will bring you love, admiration, happiness, and sex. The right "things" will keep you safe or make you into the person you really want to be. It's a plot! A plot to make one giant materialistic cult of the people of the world."

" 'They … brainwashed … plots.' Gee, Doc, and they say us cops are paranoid. You shrinks seem to be looking over your shoulders, too."

"Mike, you're not paranoid if the CIA and the FBI really are following you. And 'they' really are brainwashing you. This brainwashing complicates your life. This brainwashing makes you act in desperate ways to add to your possessions. Yeah, you know what they are doing, but it works anyway. It works until you use anti-brainwashing techniques."

"I love some good intrigue. It's like the Patty Hearst story. So, what are these anti-brainwashing techniques?"

"Patty Hearst only robbed a bank, you're robbing your life. Mike, do you remember when there used to be a lot of cults that would kidnap postadolescent kids?"

"Yeah, I remember all those phony spiritual guys. They're still around."

"Well, when kids are brainwashed by a cult, many parents got them back by kidnapping them. Then they would make the kids confront every one of the ideas that brainwashed them until they had re-programmed them. They confronted them over and over until logical thinking was automatic. You have to do the same thing. It's like re-programming a computer, except the computer weighs about eight pounds, has a lot of gooey gray stuff on the outside, and sits on your neck. The first thing we have to do to simplify your life is confront the brainwashing of the material world—the world of 'things.' "

"Doc, when the cults used to capture kids they would make them give up all their possessions. Are you saying that this cult of advertisers wants us to do the opposite? They want us to buy things and collect possessions?"

"Exactly. We buy 'things' for three reasons: to gain status, to have more fun, and to survive. It's that simple. We have been brainwashed to believe that possessions further us in these areas. To some extent they do, but not to the extreme that we have been led to believe. The problem is one of extent. We do need some things to survive. We do need some things to be happy. But do we need the right car to be seen positively by others? Do we need to drink the right beer to have friends? Do we need to smoke the right cigarette to be cool? They, the commercial makers, want us 'cult members' to believe we do. After all, no one sees a man on his horse with a nicotine patch instead of a cigarette. It wouldn't be the same. Without the cigarette company the poor schmuck wouldn't even have a name. He needs that cigarette, thus we need that cigarette."

"Doc, commercials are so obvious and stupid. I don't think they really affect me. I mean, I don't buy something just because I see a TV commercial."

"They do affect us, Mike, or there would be no commercials on TV. They sneak in feelings to overcome rational thought. Do you remember a commercial where the mother has a four-wheel drive vehicle and is trudging through snow to bring her child and his friends to a hockey match?"

Mike acknowledges.

"The opposing team doesn't make it to the match because they don't have this four-wheel drive vehicle. The opposing team has to forfeit. The "four-wheel drive" mom is the hero. She feels great. She has a heightened sense of love from her son and his friends. Her "thing"—the four-wheel drive vehicle—protected her from all kinds of turmoil. What a load of crap we are being sold. We are told that we need this vehicle so "we too" can win the status from our children. "We too" can protect them on this snowbound excursion. "We too" can be happy because the other team forfeits. We are not supposed to realize that any mom with more than a pecan for a brain would not take a carload of children out in a snowstorm. Commercials are stupid, but they work. They make us feel, not think, but feel. How much thinking is there in 'plop, plop, fizz, fizz, oh what a relief it is'? Yes, this slogan was in one of the most successful commercial ads ever because we could hear it, sense it, feel it."

"So let me get this right. Even if I recognize the stupidity of an ad, it can brainwash me. Even if I hate advertisements with a passion, they brainwash me. Even if I was the most intelligent person in the world, commercials brainwash me because they make me feel something."

"Correct. But, you can regain your own head the moment you start to take control with anti-brainwashing programming. The forces of commercialism start with a direction and take it to the extreme. They take a thing that can be useful and make it into a "need" by strongly connecting it to images, words, and feelings. They sneak up on you."

Mike started imitating a bad B movie ad.

" 'They' are in the TV. 'They' are in the magazines. 'They' make you sing when 'they' want. 'They' control your laughter. 'They' sneak up on you. You should write horror movies, Doc. You could call the first one, 'THEY.' "

"Are you finished, Mike?"

"Yeah, just a diversion, Doc."

"That reminds me of old joke about a man dying of thirst in the desert. He sees a stand about a mile away and finally crawls to it to find a salesman selling ties. The salesman tries to convince the thirsty man he needs a tie. He yells at the salesman about needing water, not a tie, then moves on until he sees another stand. The second stand is also selling ties. The first scene repeats and the thirsty man again leaves. Finally, he sees a restaurant way ahead of him. He crawls to the restaurant with his last breath, dying of thirst, and sees a sign, "No one admitted without a tie." This is what commercials try to do to us. They want us to 'buy ties in the desert.' Except when we really get to the restaurant, instead of a sign saying 'No one without a tie,' we find we *could* get into the restaurant, but we don't have enough money left for a glass of water. We do, however, have a closet full of ties."

"Doc, you're no Bill Cosby but I think I've got the idea. What they try to do is to make you believe that you have a 'need' and the possession of their 'thing' meets that 'need.' "

"Imagine what a therapy hour with Bill Cosby would cost. Anyway, that's the idea. 'Needs' must be filled, 'needs' must be met, 'needs' are essential to life. You 'need' air. You 'need' water. You 'need' food. You 'need' a four-wheel drive vehicle, to drink the right beer, to smoke the right cigarette. Did I slip those in on you? These latter objects aren't 'needs' but 'wants.' Don't confuse the fact that you 'want' a thing with the idea that you 'need' the thing. If they can get you to think you 'need' something, you'll do anything to get it. Unmet 'needs' create desperation and complications; unmet 'wants' only create mild disappointment."

"So by thinking 'need' we set ourself up to get upset. Do I do that?"

"Do you have any idea how many times you used the word 'need' in the first ten minutes of our conversation?"

"No."

"About twelve times in ten minutes. About stupid stuff like sneakers, a mistress, money."

"But there are 'needs,' aren't there?"

"In reality, your 'needs' are very few. You need to eat, drink, urinate, defecate, and find shelter in the winter. *Eat, drink, urinate, defecate, and find shelter in the winter.* Beyond those real 'needs' you have few 'needs' for objects. Yes, you may have 'needs' to act in other ways to preserve life, such as getting off the road when there is oncoming traffic. You may 'need' some objects to do your job. As a cop, you may 'need' a badge to identify yourself and a gun to protect yourself. But, your basic needs are ..."

"I know, to eat, drink, urinate, defecate, and find shelter in the winter. Most 'things' are not 'needed;' they may be 'wanted' but they are not 'needed' for either status, happiness, or to sustain life. Is that the idea?"

"It's that simple. Not necessarily easy to do, but certainly simple. Your first step toward uncomplicating your life is to fully comprehend this simple concept. Now we'll begin the programming exercises to expand your understanding and begin your anti-brainwashing. We'll go through all the exercises. Take your time so you fully understand. Start your re-programming. **Do not skip these exercises because you think you understand.** It will take actual activity to really ingrain mental programming. It will take work to simplify your life. Do your homework. Learn to sort out what really matters in your life.

EXERCISES

Exercise 1

The first re-programming exercise involves taking stock of your major possessions. I call it a "Things Inventory," and a blank copy on which you can work follows this exercise. The secret of profiting from the Things Inventory is to be thorough. Take as much time as you need, but enjoy the process.

In the first column of the inventory, you will make a simple list of your possessions and major purchases. List everything you own, everything that you've earned the money to purchase. Some people find that if they go through each room in their house and make a list, they get a more complete inventory. Then, list any major purchases that perhaps didn't end in concrete items, such as vacations, lessons of some kind, etc. Take your time. Remember to be thorough.

The next task is to decide why you own this "thing" or made this purchase. Is it a "status thing," a "happiness (fun) thing," and/or a "needs/survival thing"? Make a check in the appropriate column(s) numbered 2, 3, and 4. Most of your possessions will fall under more than one column, so check all the columns that apply. For example, a late model Porsche might be a "needs" item as a car because you use it to drive to work, but it also affords you "status" and probably "fun" if you like to drive. Be honest with yourself, particularly about the status items. People tend to be most embarrassed about status items.

Now for the scary stuff: I'd like you to think back to a time maybe 10 or 15 years ago, longer if you'd like, when you were really happy and satisfied. Then, I want you to go down your list of "things" and check those that you owned at the time. To be checked, each item must be the exact item you own now. This fifth column often makes people shiver with the realization of how few things they now own were essential to life in the past when they were happy.

In the last column, I want you to go in the other direction and check the things that you believe you will own in the same form, fifteen years from now. You will probably be surprised at how few things will have permanence.

Mike's completed Things Inventory follows your completed form. Notice the pattern. Do you see how few "things" he needed to make him happy, how few will have permanence? If you look closely, you'll begin to understand what was happening to him.

You've begun your programming when you understand why you bought your present possessions and the lack of power they really have over you. This exercise is designed to give you insight into the differences between things that are "needed" and things that are "wanted." Remember, your goal is to learn to simplify by understanding and controlling the roles "things" play in your life.

Exercise 2

This is a fun exercise where you will become aware of the "cult-like" indoctrination techniques that commercials use on us every day. I want you to look closely at a few media advertisements for the attachments and cues they use, and the effect they have on you. Most of us can't watch those cute babies or hear a heartwarming story without feeling emotion, even if we aren't inspired to run out and buy a product. Sometimes all a commercial tries to do is raise an emotion. All you have to do for this exercise is just watch a commercial and answer a few questions:

- What was the story? In what scene did the advertiser hide the product?
- What was the product being sold? Did the advertiser try to present it as better than similar products?
- What attachments did the advertiser use to provoke an emotional reaction? What were the cues for this attachment?
- What affected you the most about the commercial?
- Why is this commercial not real?

"THINGS" INVENTORY

LIST THINGS (POSSESSIONS, MAJOR PURCHASES, ETC.)	WHY DO YOU OWN? (CHECK ALL THAT APPLY)			DID YOU OWN YEARS AGO WHEN HAPPY?	WILL YOU OWN IN 10 OR 15 YEARS?
	STATUS	FUN	NEED	CHECK IF YES	CHECK IF YES
Column 1	2	3	4	5	6

"THINGS" INVENTORY

LIST THINGS (POSSESSIONS, MAJOR PURCHASES, ETC.)	WHY DO YOU OWN? (CHECK ALL THAT APPLY)			DID YOU OWN YEARS AGO WHEN HAPPY? CHECK IF YES	WILL YOU OWN IN 10 OR 15 YEARS? CHECK IF YES
	STATUS	FUN	NEED		
Column 1	2	3	4	5	6
Family car			✓		✓Some Kind
Home			✓	✓	✓
Furniture			✓		*Some maybe
Daughter's College			✓		✓
My car (sports car)	✓	✓	✓		
TV			✓	✓Owned cheaper	✓
VCR		✓			✓
Sailboat	✓	✓			?
Ranch Club Property	✓	✓			?
New deck	✓	✓			✓
Motorcycle	✓	✓			?
Kids' toys	✓	✓	some		
Fishing equipment	✓	✓			✓
Hunting equipment	✓	✓	✓		✓
Clothing	✓			✓	✓
Stereo (huge)	✓	✓			✓
Pool		✓	?		
Daughter's car		✓			
Books	✓	?			some
Home computer	✓	✓	✓		?
Knickknacks	✓				?
Pictures of family		✓			✓
Sports equipment		✓			✓
Game machine for TV	✓	✓			?
Star Trek memorabilia	✓	✓			?
Old magazines		?✓			?
Old stereo		?		✓	?
Christmas decorations	✓	✓	Some		?
Hot dog machine		?			

SESSION 3

Don't Make Your Living Room a Landfill

I remember a graduate school professor telling the class that the most important part of therapy was the relationship between the therapist and the patient. He professed that when you start liking the patient, he will start liking himself. Of course, another professor told us that having feelings for a patient would ruin objectivity, thus rendering therapy ineffective. Patients, this professor claimed, should have feelings for you, but you should be free of feelings for them. I paid for this education.

It always seems that I start to like my patients after the second session. Something happens. I've never been able to explain it. They come in with a variety of problems, often complaining, sometimes claiming that their own mothers wouldn't warn them if a grease patch were at the top of the stairs. But I guess I see something, or hear something, or just feel a connection with something inside of them that can't be explained. I like them. Out of the blue, I just seem to like them.

Mike was easy to like. He came to the third session with one of those big banana smiles. He was happy to see me. He shook my hand, creating one of those bonds between men that supersedes the usual mechanical grasp-and-squeeze handshakes amongst strangers. We connected.

"It's good to see ya, Mike."

"Yeah, it's good to see you too, Doc. I can't believe that I actually was looking forward to coming today. But don't let it go to your head."

"Ah, but do let it go to *your* head."

I still have to learn to let a good moment happen and keep my mouth shut.

22

"Your Redskins lost last weekend."

"Yeah, but Notre Dame won, so at least I'm 50-50. How was your week, Mike?"

"Great. Last Thursday I took Suzie and the kids out and we went model boat racing on the lake with a friend of mine who is really into it. It was the best time. A perfect day. Then we all went to see the new Disney movie. I think Suzie and I enjoyed it more than the kids. I need more days like that. Wait, I don't *need* them, but it *would be nice* if I had more days like that."

"Good pickup, Mike. I would have missed that one."

"Change the language and I change the feelings. See, I listened to you."

"You sure did. I guess the rock does have ears! Do you have any pictures of your wife and kids? I'd like to be able to picture them as they are when you talk about them."

Mike pulls out some pictures and starts describing his family. He tells how he and his wife met. He has cute little anecdotes to tell about each of his two children. On the bottom of the stack is a graduation picture of a pretty, high school age girl who he says nothing about.

"Who's this, Mike?"

"That's my daughter, Janelle, from my first marriage. I think I told you, she's in college now. She doesn't much like me anymore, I guess. I'm just around to pay the college tuition."

"How did you lose touch, Mike?"

"Well, it's the typical story, I guess. After I left the house I tried to keep in touch, but gradually she grew to prefer being with her friends than me. So I would just stop by every once in awhile to bring her something. I used to buy her things all the time, but they'd just end up at my house. I left a room open for her at my house, that just ended up getting filled up with toys and mementos, but no kid. Sort of looked like the rest of the house—lots of things, but little substance. Eventually, she just saw me as a person that she'd go to for money and I resented her. The battles started and we just grew apart."

"Grew apart! I hate that phrase, Mike. It makes people sound like tree branches or plants. You describe putting a bunch of junk between you and your daughter, then depict the process of 'growing apart.' "

"Maybe 'growing' apart is like what you do when you comb your hair."

"Right, Mike. We gotta work on your sense of humor a little. Now why do you think you really bought your daughter all those things?"

"OK, so maybe I provided a bunch of things for my daughter in an attempt to buy her love. Maybe it's just like we talked about in our last session where I tried to buy things to provide me with happiness or status. Deeds, not things, provide status, happiness and love. I've caused myself to 'grow apart' from what I want most out of life. I'm not sure I'm going to like all this looking at myself. Sometimes I just hate these sessions."

"I always thought that rather than use the rack or drive spikes under fingernails, a better torture would be to make people sit with a psychologist and learn how you screwed up in your life." (In my best German accent:) "You vill seet wid de shrink until you are ready to tell us all ve vant to know."

"You're a sick man, Doc. And what's worse is that I am sitting here looking to you for help."

"Mike, you said that the rest of your house was full of 'things with little substance.' What did you mean?"

"I guess we're sort of collectors. Every room is full of junk. First, the kids have every toy known to man, including every video game ever made. Then every other room has a TV, a VCR, a stereo, all electronic crap. And the knickknacks. We have so much little junk lying around it looks like a museum. There's isn't two inches of wall space that doesn't have some memento hanging on it. If we clean up it takes about five minutes to get the place messed up again. There's just barely room for all the crap we have. I guess that's not good, is it?"

"Depends on whether you want a living room or a landfill. Does the stuff make everyone happy?"

"Only just after we buy it. Just after we buy something it gets played with a lot. Or, we just sit there and admire it for awhile, then it starts being a dust collector, finally we have to buy more things to collect dust. It's like a continuous cycle of things to rely on for happiness. Renting happiness for a short period of time. Paying rent to the devil, I guess. So what do I do to break this reliance on things?"

"First let's make sure we understand the problem. With your daughter, you tried to buy her affection with purchases and became a 'buyer of things' rather than a father. You put a gap between the two of you by over-giving money, not time. You have focused on filling your home with objects in an attempt to have what is needed for happiness or status, or just to feel good. Your home has quantity, but the *quality* may be hidden by the sheer numbers of objects. Things have put a gap between you and what you want out of life."

"Sounds about right, although strange to think I could let this kind of thing happen."

"Let's discuss the job for a minute. When you go to a crime scene, and there's a lot of people and reporters around, and a lot of extra junk lying around, what's the first course of action?"

"Secure the area, clear everyone out, and determine what is evidence and what doesn't lead you anywhere."

"Do you clear even the well-intentioned people out?"

"You clear everyone out. Then you work methodically at collecting the evidence."

"Let's talk about history for a second. When my grandfather moved to Indiana and bought heavily treed land to build his farm, what do you think was the first action he took?"

"He probably cleared the land from any unnecessary trees and worked the soil. Are you trying to say the junk around my house is the trees and my relationships are the soil? I need to clear the trees and work the soil. It's all so obvious."

"Mike, I prefer if we use the term 'simple' rather than 'obvious.' I want you to constantly remember 'simpler' is almost always healthier."

"I guess I'm going to hear that word 'simple' a lot. Keep life simple. Well, I know what I have to do. I'm going to go home and call the Salvation Army and a dumpster company. I'm going to completely clean out my house, completely. Hell, I'll throw out everything except the beds. It will do my family good to live without everything for awhile. Everything goes. It will be such a free feeling to get rid of all that junk. Complete freedom. Strip the house bare. Later, after we get a few dollars, we'll buy a few essentials. I'm getting excited just thinking about it. I'll clean out the ..."

"Whoa! Beware, the sharks are in a feeding frenzy. Get the tranquilizer gun and straitjacket over here please. Calm down, Mike. You're about to destroy all the evidence, leach the soil of all its minerals. Simple is not usually extreme. Let's do this streamlining a little more moderately and logically."

"Was I getting carried away?"

"Yeah, you were getting carried away. Mike, let's do this logically, simply, calmly, methodically, reasonably, prudently, rationally ..."

"I get the idea. So you have a good vocabulary. Now, how do you suggest I start?"

" 'The ability to simplify means to eliminate the unnecessary so that the necessary may speak.' Hans Hofmann, *Search for the Real*. I like quotes. Anyway, we start by eliminating the unnecessary and useless. Let's start with the paper products around your house. Get some paper bags and let's start packing up paper to bring to a recycling place. Research suggests that 80 percent of what you file will never be seen again. Every piece of paper around the house should go under scrutiny, including books, old clippings, receipts from years ago, old newspapers, everything. Try to throw away at least three out of every four sheets of paper. Share the books, donate them or sell them if you aren't going to use them again."

"Books, now that's hard. I like to have copies of what I've read."

"I always thought that way, then I had a flood in my basement and lost about a third of my books to water damage. I was actually happy to have gotten rid of them, and I realized that if I needed any of them there was always a library. Use the natural disaster criterion to decide what to get rid of. If my books were destroyed by a natural disaster, which ones would I replace? If you wouldn't replace it, then get rid of it. What you can't get rid of pack away using some orderly system. Set a limit on the paper and books that you are going to keep out in the open."

"I don't know, Doc. I like to keep those books around just in case I run out of toilet paper. I mean, those romance novel and psychology books are probably only good as toilet paper."

"Cute, Mike. But you shouldn't be worried about wiping anywhere until you get your head out from up there, if you know what I mean."

"Ooh, you're quick. You're not going to be as easy to get one over on as the boys down at the precinct. OK, so what's after the paper? I don't think my wife and I will have any problem with throwing out a bunch of paper."

"Go through the closets and pick away at the clothes. If you haven't worn something in a year, donate it—someone else might get some use out of it. Most people find at least half of their clothes can be tossed. Next, get the kids out of the house and do the toys. As you said, most of a toy's power for enjoyment comes in the first few days of possession. Remember, a child has lived a very short life, so three months to a ten-year-old is like a year to you in sheer percentage of time. If the child hasn't touched a toy in three months, and the toy isn't seasonal like a football or baseball, store it or give it to a kid who *can* enjoy the newness. Don't try to talk the kids into it; they won't let you get rid of anything. I'm not sure any life traumas have ever been caused by a 'Chutes and Ladders' game that was given to a needy child."

" 'Chutes and Ladders' I'm not worried about, but do you mean I have to give up my bell-bottoms, Nehru jackets, and old leisure suits? Those things will come back in style, you know."

"No, you don't have to throw them out. Just wear them once a year. In fact, I'll give you ten bucks to wear bell-bottoms and a Nehru jacket to the precinct once. That'd be great! We'll take pictures and send it to one of those Hollywood TV producers for a new series, 'Nehru Cop.' Let's see, it could be about a cop with long sideburns who rides around in a '69 GTO, listening to Jimmy Hendrix tapes and saying 'groovy' to everything. Could work, could work. Do you really still keep that old stuff?"

"No, my wife played 'fashion police' when we first got married and threw out anything that I might wear that would embarrass her. I don't think we've thrown out anything since. So far I don't see any problems, but ..."

"Knickknacks and mementos."

"Now we're in trouble! I'd just as soon have the house clean with bare white walls, while Suzie thinks any bare space is a sign of poor decorating. She won't give up any of her knickknacks."

"There are two basic compromise approaches in this case. Remember, quantity reduces the impact of quality. The first is to find out what the more important pieces are, and leave those pieces out all the time. Pack the others away to bring out on special occasions, like parties and holidays. Preserve the uncluttered look the rest of the year. A second compromise for the person who likes a lot of knickknacks is to divide them according to season. Bring them out during different times of the year. In this way, the house can always look fresh, all the objects will be enjoyed, and you can enjoy the uncluttered life that will be healthier for you and your family."

"Doc, that seems like a lot of extra work. Is this going to be worth it?"

"Interestingly, psychological experiments have shown that people who are enclosed in cluttered rooms show more signs of stress than people enclosed in uncluttered rooms. Clutter saps your energy. It makes day-to-day living harder. Cluttered rooms get messier faster, causing you to have to clean up more frequently. It's actually more work to live in a cluttered home than to de-clutter and switch knick-knacks every four months. But most importantly, clutter makes your life feel more complicated. So, Mike, unclutter your living environment as a sign that you are making your life more simple. Let it be a daily reminder to think, act, and feel more simple. Put the focus on you and your relationships, not your environment."

"This is going to be a tough week of work to unclutter, Doc."

"Mike, you're pioneering, clearing land, investigating a tough case. You don't have to do everything at once, just move on it as best you can. Work steady. Don't try to do everything in one day, but do start immediately. Progress may come slowly, just like being a farmer or a cop on a crime scene. When you see the first sign of crop growth, or make the first break in the case, you'll know it was worth it."

"Doc, just one question. Do shrinks always have to use analogies and stories?"

"Funny you should ask. Therapy is like building a brick walkway—you have to lay it down brick by brick. The stories are like our ..."

"Sorry I asked, Doc. Sorry I asked."

EXERCISES

Throwing things away to unclutter your house can be a very emotional process. If you find you are having too much difficulty with the process, you haven't accepted the principles of Session 2 regarding the definition of "needs." Review that session until you have convinced yourself that you are ready to unclutter.

Before you start to unclutter you should find a number of very strong, medium-sized, empty boxes, a box of very large trash bags, and a wet rag to wipe the dust off your junk. Mark some of the boxes "donations," and some "storage." Try to keep a steady supply of boxes in case you run out. Let the garbage go in the trash bags.

Exercise 1

The first area to attack is any file cabinet, filing system, or other place where a large amount of paper has collected. Find any old papers and follow some basic rules to rid yourself of paper build-up. Some of my favorite rules are:

- Don't keep catalogs more than two months old. If you haven't ordered in two months, you probably won't.
- For that matter, don't keep magazines more than one month old. If you want articles in the magazine, cut them out and file them. Or better yet, catalog and date the topic so you can look them up in a library if necessary.
- Throw out old business letters, term papers, business cards, memos, lists, policies, outdated contracts, love letters from ex-girl/boyfriends, and so forth, that you do not need to keep for legal reasons.
- Don't save anything that you can get from a library, like newspaper clippings and cartoons. You can always catalog the dates that the cartoons or articles appeared with short descriptions of them.
- Destroy papers from long-past legal matters, such as home sales, deceased parents' tax returns, wills of deceased people, and fifteen-year-old receipts.
- Don't keep duplicates of anything. (That's why they make copiers.)
- Toss the travel brochures from those trips you wanted to take, or did take, ten years ago. Brochures change; throw them out if they are more than six months old.
- Throw out service manuals for products you don't currently own, or products you never use anymore. The toaster oven manual will long outlive the toaster oven.
- File all papers and receipts sitting on top of dressers, stairs, entertainment centers, etc. Remember, 80 percent of what you file will not be looked at again until you throw it out. I would guess that 50 percent of that remaining 20 percent is not worth keeping because you can find it easily at a library or in someone else's files. If you can toss it rather than file it, do so.

Exercise 2

Get rid of your books and back issues of magazines. Donate or give away:

- all old encyclopedias
- all old textbooks you haven't referenced in the past year and are not used in your business

- all novels, plays, or anthologies you have read, saving only one or two favorites
- any foreign language books that you can no longer can read ← typo
- outgrown children's books
- any coffee table books that have been marred by spillage or decay
- any back issues of technical magazines that are more than a year old and are not collector's items
- any picture magazine collections that you have not looked at in the past year

Store:
- any collector's items—true collector's items should be kept where they cannot be damaged when displayed
- any novels, plays, or short stories that you would like to read but don't have the time for in the next month
- any old yearbooks, picture books, or albums that you don't regularly look at
- any magazine collections used for reference

Keep on the shelf:
- books used for business or daily living reference, including magazines, and books you plan to read in the next month
- one copy of *Keeping It Simple*

Exercise 3
Attack your closets. Donate to charity:

- clothes, shoes, or jackets that have not been worn for over a year
- clothes that no longer fit (other than maternity clothes)
- children's clothes and shoes that have been outgrown
- clothes and shoes that are no longer in style
- worn out clothes and shoes you don't want to be seen in
- clothes with unremovable stains

Store:
- clothes and shoes that are out of season
- clothes and shoes that are used only for special situations (for example, tuxedos, ski clothes, green shamrock ties and leprechaun hats worn on St. Patrick's Day)

- clothes with sentimental value (i.e., wedding dresses)

Exercise 4

De-clutter your home. Throw away:

- knickknacks and mementos with no intrinsic or extrinsic value and that do not serve a purpose, like make the house smell good
- boxes whose contents you are unsure of because they haven't been opened in years
- obsolete computer equipment and business machines
- 95 percent of what's in your junk drawers and junk bins
- anything in your pantry, refrigerator, or medicine cabinet past its expiration date
- old, open bags of flour, pasta, rice, and other perishables
- all those things you saved for years thinking you'd one day find a purpose for them, like those extra pieces of wood left after you cut up that two-by-four

Give to charity:
- canned foods that you haven't opened in over a year
- duplicates that you've been saving, just in case
- toys and video games that the kids haven't played with in a long time
- furniture, musical instruments, and bric-a-brac that others may want but you didn't have the heart to throw away because they're still usable

Store:
- most of the remaining knickknacks that are left after de-cluttering
- toys and sporting equipment that are out of season
- computer equipment not in use and not obsolete

Session 4

If It Weren't for Stoplights, I'd Have No Free Time

Mike had canceled an appointment between Sessions 3 and 4. He called up and got my answering machine, then spent 15 minutes explaining why he was too busy to meet me. He told me his whole schedule: How his wife was sick, and he had to go food shopping. How the kids were sick, and he had to take them to the doctor. How he had to put in overtime on a case he was working on. The whole story of his recent life was on my answering machine. Patients always feel I have a need to know their entire schedules, in fact, even people I just meet seem to tell me their schedules. (I must have "bore me with the inane details of your life" painted on my forehead.) I wasn't really interested in Mike's schedule, unless something unusual was happening. All I cared about was that he was too booked up to be able to spend time with me.

Resistance. Now here's another term that bothers me. Many therapists figure when a patient misses an appointment or is late they are "resisting" therapy, playing a subconscious mind game. This may be true on occasion. Therapy doesn't always feel good, even though we try to make it fun. I usually find that the patients who decide to come into therapy have overbooked their lives and living has become too complicated. It's hard to fit that extra hour or two a week into an overbooked life. Once people have begun to simplify, it's amazing how much more often they attend their sessions.

I rescheduled Mike's appointment on a different day, late at night.

"Did you get my message?"
"Well, I listened to the first half hour of it, and I sort of fell asleep."
"Always a smart-ass, Doc."
"You know, Mike, in the time it took to leave that message we

could have had a session and then had a leisurely lunch, too."

"Can I help that I'm a busy man, Doc? You know, when you're as good as I am everybody wants some of your time."

"Grandiosity is a cheap fur, Mike. It won't keep you warm in the cold."

"I never heard that one before, Doc."

"I just made it up. I figure I'd prove that I could say something stupid, too. Anyway, it seems like you've been booked up a lot lately, Mike."

"Unbelievable. Like today. I got off at four. I just had some errands to run and I didn't have a chance to change."

He was still in uniform. It was 8:15 p.m. by now.

"What kind of errands, Mike?"

"Well, I had to drop my son Michael at a baseball game, and my son Kenny at karate. Then, I had to go to the cash machine, pick up the mail, and food shop. Then I dropped off the groceries at home, picked up Kenny at karate, and watched the rest of the baseball game. Then I took Michael and Kenny to get a pizza so they could eat on the way to where they were each going next. Of course, the kids have to rush and tell you everything that happened all day and they both talk at once. And all this before I could come here."

"Is that a normal day for you?"

"Pretty much!"

"Who won the game?"

"What?"

"The baseball game, who won?"

"I'm not sure, why?"

"I just like baseball, I guess. How do you feel today, Mike?"

Psychologists always ask questions when we already know the answers. By now, I've noticed the strained look in Mike's eyes, the fidgetiness. He's traveling at a hundred miles an hour, sitting still, but I just had to ask. I get a strange satisfaction in asking these kinds of questions—therapy is an unusual occupation.

Mike laughs. "How do I feel? I don't have time to think about how I feel. Between the overtime, the kids, everybody wanting me to be responsible, my wife feeling she needs a break until she becomes useless after awhile, I just try to keep everyone happy. Then the sprinkler system needs to be blown out, and I need to bring in all the summer yard stuff for the winter; the cars need ..."

He would have gone on for the full hour if I didn't stop him. I remember when I was in graduate school a well-known psychologist said that his patients were all "whining, sniveling cowards" until he taught them to think rationally. Whenever someone starts to go off like Mike, I beacon back to that phrase for just a moment, even though I don't like the idea of being so degrading and judgmental. We humans sure do complain a lot about the lives we build for ourselves.

(*Interrupting*) "Hey, Mike."

"Yeah."

"Did I ever tell you about how hectic the day of a psychologist can be? Today, I had to deal with two emergencies even before I got to work. Not real emergencies, but potential emergencies. Then, I worked out ..."

"There's a lesson in this, isn't there, Doc? Why don't you just come out and say it instead of playing around?"

"OK, Mike. Shut up, quit your whining, chill out, calm down, loosen up, and all that stuff."

Mike has a deep belly laugh for about thirty seconds.

"Now I've heard it all. My own shrink is telling me to shut up. I guess I'm a pretty sad case."

"You just need a crack in the head every once in awhile. Mike, with your schedule, do you ever just get to relax, kick back, and let time pass without packing it solid with activity?"

"Never! If it weren't for stoplights, I'd have no free time. On top of it all, I had to de-clutter last week, remember? It actually took me two weeks to do what should have taken me a couple of days."

"Then we're going to have to learn about de-cluttering 'time,' also. Misuse of time overcomplicates our lives."

"OK, here we go. Once you use the word 'simple' or the word 'complicated,' I know the lessons are about to begin."

"How perceptive. Maybe this anti-brainwashing has started to take effect. Mike, I'd like you to try a little experiment with me. Close your eyes for a second, listen to this tape, and just concentrate on breathing in and out smoothly. Hold on ... now close."

I played him a soothing tape of classical music for a minute.

"Mike, how long did you have your eyes closed?"

"About 25 or 30 seconds."

"Now, I want you to close your eyes the same way and talk to me about this week's schedule."

Mike obediently rambles on for about twenty seconds.

"How long were you talking about your schedule?"

"I don't know, about a minute or two, maybe a little longer. So what's the point?"

"You listened to music for a minute on a tape and thought it was 30 seconds, then you talked about your schedule for less than 30 seconds and thought it was a minute or two. So if we are doing something pleasant, time goes faster and ..."

"If we do something unpleasant, time goes slower. Everyone knows that. What's the big deal?"

"Do you want time to go slower or faster?"

"Well, time goes too fast for me now, so I guess I want it to go slower. So are you saying I purposely pack it solid with things to do so time will go slower?"

"I'm not saying anything, just pointing something out. Does that fit?"

"No, because I like to be busy at work because time goes faster. So that shoots that theory."

Mike is very proud to have proved me wrong.

"You're right, shoots that theory. Unless you are saying that it is unpleasant to be sitting around with nothing to do. Packed-solid time isn't always the least pleasant option. Remember, I said unpleasant time goes slower, not 'unbusy' time."

"Well, do you think it's pleasant dealing with emergencies all the time—blood, accidents, people who are victims and those kinds of things?"

"Would you rather be busy, or sit around in the sector car or at the precinct doing nothing?"

"No, I'd rather be busy."

"Then I guess it's more pleasant to be busy, even if it's blood and guts because time goes faster, right?"

"Okay, I'll give you that one. You win. But ..."

"Mike, 'you'll give me that one'—should I be keeping score? I thought we were on the same team."

"Just an expression, Doc. Don't take it personally. Besides, I wouldn't give you one if I didn't think I could beat you later on."

"I'm not worried, Mike. You won't have time to beat me later on."

"Good comeback. I'll give you half on that one."

"Let me make sure you have this, Mike. You pack your time solid because you are convinced it is more pleasant to be busy than not to be busy. It's the same as convincing yourself that it's better to live complicated than live simply. If you could appreciate unbusy time, you might feel differently. Unbusy time is simpler, but you have convinced yourself it's less pleasant. Yet you whine about being too busy."

"So you're saying that I'm convincing myself to do exactly what I do not want, pack my time solid. However, when I go hunting I enjoy the unbusy time of just sitting in the woods. It's even better sometimes than the shooting part."

"It sounds almost like you need to have permission to be unbusy before you can enjoy it, Mike."

"Could be. So you're suggesting that in order to live simply I have to first understand that I can leave space in my schedule to do nothing and learn to enjoy that kind of time. I'm not sure that I don't enjoy unbusy time."

"You don't act that way. The rest of it you've got right on. Using time effectively will mean cutting back on activities to allow free time to gain a measure of enjoyment. Simplicity means that enjoyment time is more focused on the important parts of life, like the people you care about, relaxing, those sorts of things."

"But the problem I have with all this is that I don't feel I have control over my own time. How am I supposed to learn to use time effectively when everyone else seems to schedule my time for me? Like today."

"Time that is full of obligations is more complicated. Most obligations are usually entered into without concern for time. We have the choice, and we don't always view time as part of that choice. If an obligation is far enough in advance, we usually agree to it believing that our time will 'loosen up' by then. It doesn't, so we're in trouble. Do you make time choices as carefully as you do money choices?"

"What do you mean?"

"Do you think about committing your time, say eight hours this month, as much as you would making a $300 purchase of, say, a car stereo or a bracelet for your wife?"

"No, money is really tight right now. Three hundred dollars is a lot."

Mike stares away for a pensive moment before he collects his thoughts.

"I guess *time* is tight too. You were supposed to make me feel better today, Doc."

"Our session's not over yet."

By the way, a trip to the therapist doesn't always make you feel better unless you walk away with some hope for change—some idea of direction. That's why there are exercises at the end of every chapter in this book.

"Doc, who was it that said time is money?"

"I think it was Ben Franklin, and basically he meant that with time you could earn money. But, you know, it's interesting—the reverse is not true. Money is not time. I always think it's revealing to ask someone what he would do if he won millions in the lottery. All of a sudden, the focus of life is how to spend and enjoy your time. If you tell a person he has a disease and is going to die soon, his focus will be on how he is going to spend and enjoy his time. Money is unimportant in extremely good or bad situations—when life is on the line. Yet, we are so willing to give up time to enjoy if special conditions like these don't prevail. Time is our most valuable commodity, even if conditions don't cause us to emphasize it."

"I have so many responsibilities. Like my mom. She was in a car accident and I take care of her now. Things like that just eat time away."

"It's a strange thing about obligations like your mom. Your brothers and sisters don't have to do anything for your mom because you rush in there and take the responsibility. You make life easier for everyone else by complicating yours. We have to work to control *your* time first, then figure out what needs to be done and how to do it. Remember, we want to look at how you spend your time first, since it is the most valuable asset of your life."

"So, how do I control time when it seems to control me?"

"First, you make time choices simpler. Let's start to think of everything in terms of time. Every new obligation we will think of in terms of time. Every new activity for the kids will be thought of in terms of time. Every new purchase will be thought of in terms of time. We will look at the pleasantness of an activity. We will look at choices that will make time more pleasant. If time is spent pleasantly you will be more involved, more engaged. Even your kids will enjoy life more if they aren't always running from place to place. We have to put quality back into you and your children's time."

"I spend a lot of time with my kids. I was with them from work until I came here."

"Yes, but we want time that has quality—simpler time. We want time where you are more involved in their lives, not just a robot-like transporter, provider, rulemaker, and homework machine. We want time where you are a dad, not just a cabby."

"I resent that."

"Mike, you just don't seem to treat yourself well when it comes to your time. You are time starved. You wouldn't think of starving your body of good food, but you'll starve yourself of good time. You're like the guy who eats a lot of food, but nothing with any nutrients. You fill your time solid with obligations. This makes time go slower, but it's not pleasant, and not good for you. Making time go slower is not a healthy goal in life."

"I resent being called just a cabby. I am very involved with my kids."

"Who won the game?"

"What?" Mike starts getting angry.

"Your son's baseball game, who won?"

"I TOLD YOU, I DON'T ... know (*he has a moment of insight*) ... OK, crack me upside the head again ... Doc, do me a favor. Shut up!" *Mike laughs.*

EXERCISE

Long ago, someone put a stick in the ground and started measuring the sun around a circle. Before that, our ancestors' stomachs growled for dinner time, and they slept when they were tired—sometimes four hours, sometimes eight hours, sometimes ten. Timekeeping is man's augmentation to nature, a pervasive, complicated system that is now

r[...] to society. Time is like all the systems man created: if you
[...]ol it, it will control you.

[...]n time is a problem for people, they are often taught to man-
a[...]ir time better, sort of a "get organized" approach to therapy. In
t[...]cess, they learn to make lists, set goals, prioritize, not procrasti-
n[...] etc. Strangely enough, I have observed that people can use good
time management skills to schedule a lot more activity than they are
ever capable of doing. You need to cut back activity to manage time,
not just make lists and schedules to organize time. Cutting back is difficult, but a key to happiness—it will be a tough project.

Mike was asked to complete the following exercise to understand
the importance of time. I'd like you to do it, too.

1. Make a time log over the course of a two-week period. After your
    time log is complete, look closely at your time and break it down
    into *work time, time given to others, and time given to self. Work time*
    includes time spent earning a living and time spent in housekeeping
    ta[..]s. *Time given to others* includes errands for family members, and
    the time you spend meeting other personal commitments. *Time for
    self* includes time left open for your own pleasure. Ignore sleep time.
    Figure your totals for each category. A copy of Mike's two-week
    chart appears at the end of this chapter.

2. Now construct a more ideal version of your time log. (A copy of
    Mike's ideal version follows his actual one at the end of this chap-
    ter.) Be realistic, since you still have to work, but leave a reasonable
    amount of time for yourself, generally around two hours per work
    day, six hours on non-work days. In Mike's case, he complained
    that leaving this time was not possible. He had some difficulty with
    the concept that he could spend time with his children doing some-
    thing he wants to do, as opposed to always meeting their needs.
    Remember that time for yourself does not always mean being alone
    or separate from the ones you love.

3. After you have constructed this ideal chart, I'd like you to set goals
    heading in the direction of your ideal time log. Looking at Mike's
    ideal chart, you will see that he set goals to exercise at a local gym
    three times a week and to go out with his wife for five hours without
    his "responsibilities" once a week. No talk of the children. He also

decided to involve the children in an activity he want█████████he night a week. In order to accommodate these activities,█████cut back on some overtime and some of his children's extr█████ties. He was surprised when children raised a fuss at first, bu█████d that they adapted very quickly to the new schedule. As Mi█████t back and focused on himself, the quality of time spent with the███l-dren was greatly improved.

Other typical goals you might set include:
- spending three nights a week and one weekend day at home with the family
- playing golf once a week
- spending one night a week with friends
- dining out with your children once or twice a week
- staying late at the office only two nights a week instead of four
- finding time to read at least one book a week, even if it means locking your bedroom door
- enjoying a romantic dinner at a nice restaurant with your significant other once a week
- phasing out a second job

4. Once you have established your new goals and have constructed your ideal chart, it's time to start living without a schedule. If you have so much activity that you still need to look at a calendar once a day, then your schedule needs to be reduced even further (with the exception of work schedules). Mike found that he still had trouble remembering what to do every day, so he made a couple of further cuts until he only needed to look at the calendar once a day, instead of every hour or so. I also told Mike that he had to be able to go without a watch at least one day a week. While this took even greater reduction, his watch-less days tended to be the ones he most enjoyed.

5. Finally, as Mike did, you must learn to look at money purchases in terms of time. Looking at the time-costs of buying a "thing" is very important in understanding what possessions will actually enhance your life, and what possessions will actually detract from your life. Time-consuming possessions are usually those that detract from enjoying life.

New purchases should be looked at as time-based decisions. I call this decision making process my "pleasure-rich formula:" Will the time spent enjoying a possession be greater than the time spent working to pay for it, worrying about it, working on it, and working to pay for the maintenance of it? Next, will the time you spend using the possession, working to buy it, or keep it maintained severely detract from your time enjoying the important people in your life? Finally, would you willingly shorten your life by the amount of time it will take to have and keep this possession? Because, in essence, you are making a decision to sacrifice a part of your life every time you buy a new possession. If the answer to each of these questions is "yes," the possession potentially is pleasure-rich. If the answer at any point is "no," then you are looking at a pleasure-deficient "thing" that will complicate your life rather than make you happy.

When figuring your "pleasure-rich formula" take into account not only how you feel about an object now, but also how you will feel about the object in the future. An interesting observation about "things" is that they are most enjoyable when they are new and maintenance free. They bring the least pleasure when they cost the most in upkeep. So when deciding "pleasure-richness," consider the time costs both at the beginning and at the end of the use of the possession.

Boats are, I believe, a prime example of how "pleasure-rich formulas" can be demonstrated. Many people with whom I work would love to own a boat. They claim they *need* the stress relief that a day on the ocean or the Long Island Sound can give them. They also claim that their families are excited about spending time on the water, so they won't lose family time. They rationalize that a boat will increase their enjoyment of life tenfold. And for some it does.

But since many people do not make phenomenal salaries, buying a boat will require sacrifices. And depending on the type of boat, those sacrifices can make the "pleasure-richness formula" very revealing. The time costs of a boat include time to earn money to buy the boat, time to earn money for maintaining the engine, painting, scraping off barnacles, winterizing, summer-izing, making sails (if a sailboat) and docking, mooring, and trailering costs. Much time is spent either working on the boat yourself or working to earn the money to hire someone to work on it. This adds up to a heavy work time expenditure that must be counterbalanced by pleasure time actually spent on the water.

In the first years of owning a boat, many of my patients have found that time spent on the boat is counterbalanced by the time expense of maintaining the boat. The boat is "pleasure-rich" because it provides more pleasure than it takes in work effort. But after a couple of years the newness of the boat wears off and maintenance costs increase. The family tires a little of the days on the water and gets involved in other pursuits. Dad is testy on the boat now because he recognizes this "thing" that he is working so hard to keep is not bringing the enjoyment it used to. Quickly the boat moves to a "pleasure-deficient" position. I suggest to these boat owners that they sell the boat as soon as they reach this pleasure-deficient state. It has become a complicated "thing" that will only drain them of life's energy and time. Most people won't listen to me at first when I suggest that they sell, because they refuse to believe that their glory days of boating and pleasure-richness are over, or they don't want to lose a few bucks on the boat. But when their lives get so complicated they can't stand it anymore, then they listen.

Of course, this does not happen to all boat owners. For some people, boating becomes a foundation that brings them steady happiness throughout their lives. However, when this is not the case, be aware of the changing nature of the "pleasure-richness formula." There is an old saying that the two happiest days in a boater's life are the day he buys his boat and the day he sells it. Complicated, "pleasure-deficient" possessions bring the most happiness when they disappear.

Be aware when you are determining something's "pleasure-richness," that some pleasures, like a vacation, actually bring enjoyment for longer than the length of the trip. The anticipation of a trip is pleasurable, as is the reliving of the experience. Children will often remember a family vacation long into their adult lives, but forget about an expensive Christmas present after a few months. Sometimes working on a possession is also pleasurable, such as mechanics who like to restore old cars. To be fair in making judgments, include less tangible factors, like memories and on-going enjoyment of fixing something when figuring the time of pleasure.

Just a final note on the "pleasure-rich formula": I am not suggesting that all possessions for all people become pleasure-deficient after a while. Be aware that there are two sides to the "pleasure-rich formulas"—the cost in time of maintaining the possession and the enjoyment time of the possession. The cost in time is closely related to the value of your time in the marketplace as determined by society. Someone making $15 an hour must work more time to earn a $5,000 boat than someone making $100 an hour. The formula changes depending on income level. It is easy for a wealthy person to pay others to work on the boat and thus make possessing it simpler. Unfortunately, in today's materialistic society we have succumbed to the belief that we should live as "high" a lifestyle as we can. So, what often happens is that the person who can't afford to buy a $5,000 boat buys it anyway, and the person who *can afford* the $5,000 boat buys a $20,000 boat that he can barely afford. Both could have kept it simple, but complicated their lives instead. Both are equally in trouble.

TIME LOG

DAY / DATE	WHAT WAS THE ACTIVITY?	AMOUNT OF TIME SPENT IN ACTIVITY	HOW WAS TIME SPENT? WORKING ON OTHERS / ON SELF

MIKE'S TIME LOG—REAL

DAY / DATE	WHAT WAS THE ACTIVITY?	AMOUNT OF TIME SPENT IN ACTIVITY	HOW WAS TIME SPENT? WORKING ON OTHERS / ON SELF
Monday 3/21	Breakfast/Getting Ready	1 1/2 hrs	work / self
Monday 3/21	Drive to work	1/2 hr	work
Monday 3/21	Work	9 1/2 hrs	work
Monday 3/21	Conversation & lunch	1/2 hr	Self / Others
Monday 3/21	Dinner & take care kids	2 1/2 hrs	Others
Monday 3/21	Pay bills	1 hr	work
Monday 3/21	Watch TV talk to wife	1 hr	Self
Went	to	Bed	
Tuesday	Breakfast & get ready	1 1/2 hrs	work
Tuesday	Drive & work	11 hrs	work
Tuesday	Dinner alone	45 min	Self
Tuesday	Kids home put to bed	1 1/2 hrs	Others
Tuesday	Talk with Suzie	1/2 hr	Self
Tuesday	Fix busted sink	1/2 hr	work
Went	to	Bed	

MIKE'S TIME LOG—IDEAL

DAY / DATE	WHAT WAS THE ACTIVITY?	AMOUNT OF TIME SPENT IN ACTIVITY	HOW WAS TIME SPENT? WORKING ON OTHERS / ON SELF
	Workout	1/2 to 1 hr	Self
	Leisurely Breakfast	1 hr	Self, family
	Work	4 hrs	work
	Play with kids	1 1/2 hrs	Self & others
	Wife & I go out to dinner	2 1/2 hrs	Self
	Meet up with friends	2 hrs	Self
	Home to put kids to bed	1 hr	Others
	Watch tv, read & relax	2 hrs	Self & wife
	Romance	1 hr	Self & wife
	Sleep		

SESSION 5

A Balanced Checkbook is of Little Use if You Can't Lift It

I've read that people are more likely to be honest about their sex lives than their finances. When I ask a patient to bring in his financial information, I often get a series of questions like "Why do you need to get into that part of my life?" "Are you worried about getting paid?" "Do we have to discuss finances?"

Mike was not so resistant. In fact, his only comment was "If you could figure out how to simplify them, you are a magician." The reality is that most people have too little training in handling finances, which leads to complications.

Mike entered the next session carrying a box chock-full of loose papers, checkbook ledgers, and receipts. He had a strange grin on his face, like a kid who knows he's eaten the last cookie and is going to get in trouble for it.

"OK, Mike, what's the look?"

"I hate this stuff. I pay the bills and balance the checkbook once a month for a night or two and every time I get really upset and depressed. On my way here, I was just imagining what you were going to say."

"I'll take that to mean this stuff is a real mess. Is that some cooked egg I see in there with the rest of the papers? Just kidding. I'm looking forward to this. I love cleaning out the complicated stuff. Let's start by looking at your checkbook ledger."

Mike hands me a wallet-size checkbook ledger with the year and his name written on the front. The first thing I notice is the number of checks he's written each month. At quick glance there was only an average of 14 or 15 written during the last couple of months.

"Mike, this isn't so bad. I expected much worse given the way you were talking."

"Yeah, that one isn't so bad."

I missed his hint completely.

"Mike, which one of these checks is your rent and utilities? I saw a couple of checks to banks, but couldn't tell what they were for."

"Uh, it's not in that checkbook."

He hands me another larger checkbook with the year and the word "household" written on it.

"Uh-oh, I am seriously afraid of the answer to this next question. How many of these checkbooks are there in total?"

"Seven, but I hardly ever use one of them."

Mike puts seven checkbooks of varying sizes on the table, with volumes of checkbook ledgers. All I could do was shake my head and smile.

"At least they're all balanced," Mike says with that cookie-stealing grin.

"A balanced checkbook is of little use if you can't lift it. Why do you have so many checkbooks?"

"Well, one is mine, one is for the house. My wife has one. One is a saving account that we need to use money from every once in awhile, so we got one of those checking-with-interest accounts. One we used for a business that we had once. We closed the business, but there is still some money in it. And I keep a joint one with my mother of money that she gave me as a gift, but I don't want to spend it as long as she's alive. Finally, one is an old account that we use in emergencies, or for Christmas, vacations, or for some extras that the kids might need."

"Damn, I could probably re-shingle my roof with just six months of your bank statements. Let me guess, you use a direct deposit of your paychecks so that a little goes in each account."

"Well, I direct deposit into three of the accounts—the household, savings, and emergency account. Some of my mom's social security check goes into her account, and my holiday and uniform checks go into my account. My wife puts her own money into her account from somewhere."

"What happens when one of the kids needs a $10 check for a school field trip?"

"Depends on who he asks. It could come out of any of the accounts depending on which one has the money at the time. I told you it was a mess."

"A mess is being a little kind to yourself. With all the paper you use in your checking, you probably have single-handedly created a national overdependence on Canada for lumber. Mike, do you realize that with all the checkbooks combined you write 35 to 50 checks a month?"

"Sounds about right. So how many checkbook jokes am I going to have to suffer through?"

"I got a bunch. You know, Mike, I could probably dunk a basketball without moving if I stood on top of these checkbooks and I'm only five-ten."

"I get it—this is aversive conditioning. Every time I write a check now I'm going to think of your jokes and get sick to my stomach."

"Speaking of aversive conditioning, you just told me you don't like to write checks, yet you do it 35 to 50 times a month. Think of all that time that you're using up. If I don't like doing something I try to spend less time doing it."

"Well, ya gotta pay for things, boss." *Mike says this in his best Tom Sawyer accent.* "How many checks should I be writing?"

"Under ten!"

"Are you serious?"

"Under ten checks a month from only one checkbook. Under seven if you can get there. Or under five if you really want a simple life. Over twenty and you might as well sign your soul over to the complications devil. You might as well give yourself up to the fourth circle of Dante's Inferno. You might just as well …

"I get the idea. Actually, I don't know what in hell you are talking about on that last one—Dante's Inferno. Sounds like you're getting carried away."

"Dante was this Italian writer, artist, and poet who wrote about the nine circles of hell, representing the vices that get people to hell. The fourth circle was for people who misused money and property."

"What were the other circles of hell?"

"The first was for people who were not baptized, the second for people who give in to carnal lust, the third for gluttons, the fourth ..."

"Stop there, Doc. Sounds like you're telling my life story. It's a little scary. I better hold off on the spiritual stuff until later. Let's see now, Dante was in the Middle Ages, so this simple stuff was not new then. It's an old-time concept."

"As Dante said, 'He must go backwards, who would most advance.' Simplifying life is a concept that goes back way before Dante, in the ancient Japanese and Chinese philosophies of Tao and Zen, in the writing of Plato and Aristotle, in just about every religion, through to Jefferson, Franklin, Ghandi, and King. I personally believe most intelligent people begin to understand that a simpler life is a better life as they get older and wiser. We're just trying to get you to realize it now and work to make your life better."

"So let me get this right. You're just trying to take credit for this stuff that all these dead guys said long ago."

"You're really good, Mike. You've gotten me completely off the track so you don't have to deal with the checkbook stuff. I remember trying to sidetrack the teacher when I was in school. You are really a master at it. Now let's get back to work."

"If there's one thing you learn as a cop, it's how to bullshit. OK, how in the world are you going to get me under ten checks?"

"Let's start by listing out what the checks are for. First, what are the essentials? Like the mortgage, utilities, phone ..."

"Well, I've got a mortgage, of course, the phone, electricity and gas, oil for heat, a car loan, equity loan, credit cards ..."

"Stop! A car loan, equity loan, and credit cards are not the essentials. We'll list them as credit. Go on."

"Well, there's a loan on a piece of property in North Carolina, and taxes and administration fees for the property. I guess that's credit. Then there's a bunch of expenses for the kids that come up every month, clothes, that kind of stuff. There's checks to the grocery store, visits to the automatic teller machine when we remember to write them in ..."

Mike was starting to turn green. I couldn't help but laugh a little.

"You look like you just ate a 400-pound burrito and can't pass gas."
Mike laughs. "I told you I hate this stuff."

"Let's start to simplify. First, I want you to close all the checking accounts except one. Turn the others into *one* savings account, or just close them. And I want all your accounts at the one bank that you can trust the most."

"One bank! What's that got to do with anything? I keep them in four banks on purpose. Just in case one closes."

"One bank, Mike. Pick a trustworthy bank. Make sure your money is insured. Get to know someone there, so you have a name to call in case you want to do a transaction. Diversity in accounts is for people with a lot more money than you. It's more important for you to simplify right now."

"What's the difference if the money's in checking or savings accounts?"

"Savings accounts will force you to use cash more often rather than writing a check. A savings account is a different mentality. If you need a check, transfer the money to the checking or just plain use cash. It's much simpler. Besides, you won't have to build another addition on your house for those checkbooks."

"Very funny. Well, if I'm going to use cash than I'll end up using the cash machine more often."

"Wrong idea. I want the cash cards locked away only for an emergency, maybe once or twice a year. For goodness sake, get them out of your wallet and out of your wife's purse. Cash machines are severe complicators of finances. Keep a reserve of cash on hand instead of writing checks for that field trip in school."

"This isn't going to be easy. What do I do about ... How do I go about ... I know what you are going to tell me before I even ask the question. You just want my banking as simple as possible. Everything in one place. Not spread out. What else?"

"Well, we're going to leave the essentials alone. That's the mortgage, oil, electric, and phone. You usually need a check for them."

"Okay. Next."

"Credit. Credit is the ultimate complicator of possessions. Remember, the amount of time you spend earning a possession is directly proportionate to the amount of credit you use."

"We all have to have credit. Our world runs on credit."

"Mike, I'm going to let you in on the history of credit. In the Middle Ages, the rich lord invented credit as a way to take over the property of others and gain greater riches. The lords would charge interest rates on necessities that were not affordable and eventually would bring about the downfall of the landowners, thus forcing them to surrender their property back to the lord. The lords would then let the ex-landowners stay and work the land, but only give them a small piece of the profit. It was an enslaving process. Credit today is still an enslaving process. We get into credit binds and all of a sudden we are working for a bank or credit card company. If you pay the minimum on a credit card with high interest it can take up to ten years to pay it off. That's slavery to a dinner you ate ten years ago. Not a good idea. The worse part is, most of us fall into it."

"You know, Doc, I can't tell you how many times I've gotten a paycheck and didn't see a penny of it because I was paying off bills. How do you get out?"

"First, list your creditors in order of how much you owe each one. Now I want you to pick one charge card that you have to pay every month. Cancel the rest of your plastic. Only use the charge card in emergencies."

"Can't I keep one other credit card?"

"You can do what you want. Ideally, keep only a charge card. Sometimes frequent travelers benefit from an infrequently-used credit card. Next, I want you to either consolidate all your creditors into one payment, or take the smallest credit amount on your list and start to pay it off. Pay the minimums on the rest and start paying off the creditors one by one. No more charging unless you can pay it off immediately and need a tax record. Forget about saving for awhile. Your first project is to work out a plan to pay off the creditors."

"If I consolidate, what should I look for?"

"Look for a low-interest loan that you can pay a reasonable amount that won't hurt you each month. Try to double up on payments as quickly as possible. You have 12 checks going to credit cards and the like. I want that down to as few as possible, if not just one."

"What else can be done?"

"What are these Ranch Club checks for?"

"Well, my wife and I bought this property in North Carolina about seven years ago. We got a loan, which right now we only pay the interest on. We also pay a monthly administration fee for upkeep and a yearly tax bill. It was an investment that just didn't turn out too well yet."

"Is there a house on it? How much is it worth on the market?"

"There's no house. We were going to build, but we haven't yet. It's not worth much now, in fact, we might even lose a few thousand dollars if we sold now. It should go up as soon as the rest of the community sells out."

"What's it got? Like horses and pretty trees and a lake and all that fun stuff."

"It's really nice. Log cabins all around. You can ride the horses, hike, go fishing. It's a great place, real resort-like. We visited the property a couple of times and had a pretty good time. Of course, we stayed in a hotel. But the Ranch Club people are real nice, and they think it will turn around soon."

"Got suckered, didn't you?"

"Yup."

"That's a pleasure-deficient possession, all right. Cut your losses, immediately. Right now you've paid for the property two times over, and you still don't own it. You're not ready for a second house. Upkeep is more than a yearly vacation would cost you. The money you put into the Ranch Club alone would get you out of debt in two years. Sell it. Take the loss."

"That's not easy. We've thought about it, but have never gotten around to it."

"Mike, it becomes a pride thing not to lose money on an investment. That's how people make bad decisions. They don't cut their losses. Remember Dante, 'He must go backwards, who would most advance.' Sell it tomorrow. Even if you lose a few grand, you'll be even after six months. Remember your last session. Don't put any more of your valuable time into earning money to pay for something you are not using. Do you want to sacrifice a part of your life for the Ranch Club?"

"This simplifying is a lot of work!"

"Not as much as carrying around those damned checkbooks. Anyway, imagine: You sit down to do your bills. You write five to seven checks, seal the envelopes, put stamps on and you're done for the month."

"That sounds too good to be true."

"And, once that is established, it takes no work to maintain. Getting to a simple life is hard both mentally and physically. Staying there makes life very stress-free. As for the rest of what you're writing checks for, I want you to use cash whenever possible. If your charge card can be paid at the bank, I even want you to use cash there. Cash for groceries, cash for gas, cash to school. Overdo the use of cash rather than checks or plastic at first, until it becomes habit. We've just reduced your check writing to under twenty. We've helped you escape the complication demons, we've lifted you out of the Inferno. In a few months, once you've simplified, you'll be amazed how the monthly bill-paying session will almost feel good."

"But Doc, what am I going to do with all these old checkbooks?"

"Are you feeding me a straight line, Mike?"

"Yeah, what the hell, I thought I'd get one more checkbook joke out of you."

"Okay, let's see ..."

EXERCISE

The following pages show Mike's checkbook ledgers, lists of creditors, and a breakdown of the two ways Mike reduced his check writing. By following the next five steps, you will be able to reduce your check writing as well. Remember, the idea is to control your flow of money so that your life is more simple. Everybody's situation is different, so don't expect every single technique Mike used to apply to you. The general principle will, however, help you simplify your finances, and thus your life.

1. Take your checkbook ledgers for the last three months and place the entries into categories of what the checks paid. The categories Mike used were essentials, creditors, and daily living expenses. "Essentials" are expenses that must be paid by check and are need-ed to live. Notice that Mike listed cleaning of uniforms as a daily living expense even though this is a requirement of his work, because it is not an essential that absolutely had to be paid by check.

2. Figure out how much cash you need on the average to cover your daily living expenses each week or every two weeks. Work out a sys-tem to keep that amount of cash, plus 20 percent, in storage in your home, either in a safe or a locked box. Try to keep from going to the bank more than once a week, every two weeks if possible. And try to make bank withdrawals somewhat methodical. It is important that you have a good idea of how this system will work; making the withdrawals methodical will aid in testing the system.

3. Cut your losses on any pleasure-deficient possessions that you owe money on. Sell them or do whatever you can to eliminate debt on things that you don't need or don't enjoy enough to justify the time you spend paying for them. Don't let your ego get in the way of cutting your losses! People who take risks probably make at least a couple bad business decisions in their lifetimes. Don't continue to make bad decisions by supporting things that cost you days or months of your vaulable time.

4. Fill in the worksheet for consolidation or payoff of loans. It gives two scenarios—either consolidating your other debt or paying off creditors one by one. Notice that on the worksheet you are to work out a plan over the course of a year. Sometimes the best way to control your creditors is to use a combination of the two techniques. Remember, the goal is to reduce the number of checks you write to as few as possible. Follow the course that Mike has taken through his answers to the worksheets.

5. The final step is to go back to the original list of your checkbook ledger entries and copy down the entries that you will not be eliminating in your long-range plan. Make sure this number is as low as possible.

* * * * *

In the course of controlling the flow of money in your life, you will undoubtedly face many setbacks and problems. Do not stop if you find that things aren't going smoothly. Simplifying your life will not be an entirely smooth process—it is unnatural for you if have lived a complicated life for a long time. Once a setback occurs, just start over where you left off. Remember, "He must go backwards, who would most advance."

MIKE'S CHECKBOOK LEDGER—ONE MONTH

Payee	Amount
Electric company	231.20

School field trip	22.00
Cash	100.00
Little League	36.00
Garage	212.00
Joe Brown	20.00
Mortgage	796.00
Record club	22.95
Grocery store	128.37
Precinct golf tournament	65.00
Retirement gift donation	20.00
Mike's VISA card	85.00
MasterCard	65.00
Sports store	59.24
Boat loan	136.40
Cash	125.00
Grocery store	95.62
American Express	126.34
Ranch Club	257.00
Sears credit card	32.00
Hardware store	22.36
J.C. Penney's credit card	35.00
Dentist	75.00
Fitness club	25.00
Student loan	115.88
Restaurant	37.56
Grocery store	107.69
Phone bill	62.21
Cable TV	34.50
Hairdresser	33.00
Deli foods	18.65
Cash	100.00
Newspaper	16.50
Girl Scout cookies	28.00
Drugstore	36.41
Local store credit card	42.36
Grocery store	156.34
Hardware store	44.88
Dry cleaning for uniforms	42.35
Cash	100.00

Suzie's VISA card	97.61
Video store	22.15
Library—overdue books	2.35

CATEGORIZING MIKE'S CHECKS

Essentials

Electric company	231.20
Mortgage	796.00
Phone bill	62.21

Daily Living

Cable TV	34.50
School field trip	22.00
Cash	100.00
Little League	36.00
Garage	212.00
Joe Brown	20.00
Sports store	59.24
Cash	125.00
Grocery store	95.62
Hardware store	22.36
Dentist	75.00
Fitness club	25.00
Restaurant	37.56
Grocery store	128.37
Record club	22.95
Grocery store	128.37
Precinct golf tournament	65.00
Retirement gift donation	20.00
Hairdresser	33.00
Deli foods	18.65
Cash	100.00
Newspaper	16.50
Girl Scout cookies	28.00
Drugstore	36.41
Grocery store	156.34
Hardware store	44.88

Dry cleaning for uniforms		42.35
Cash		100.00
Video store		22.15
Library—overdue books		2.35

Credit	Monthly	Total Owed
Mike's VISA Card	85.00	1,255.00
MasterCard	65.00	724.84
American Express	126.34	
Ranch Club	257.00	16,859.00
Sears credit card	32.00	326.20
J.C. Penney's credit card	35.00	381.06
Student loan	115.88	1,234.68
Local store credit card	42.36	444.91
Suzie's VISA card	97.60	2,524.07
Boat loan	136.40	5,019.22

MIKE'S SOLUTION TO WRITING LESS CHECKS

Contine to pay by check

Electric company	231.20
Mortgage	796.00
Phone bill	62.21
Cabe TV	34.50
School field trip	22.00

(They didn't want their child to carry this amount of money yet)

American Express	126.34

(The decision was made to keep an American Express card because it forced a full payment to be made each month)

Daily Living Expenses

The decision was made to pay for rest of daily living expenses in cash which requires a withdrawal on a set schedule of the average amount spent each month plus 20%. The average monthly amount was around $2,100. The decision was made to withdraw $525 each Monday in cash, plus anticipated extras for the week. (Often once people adjust to spending cash, the money they spend on their living expenses goes down.)

Credit

These bills were paid off from savings, then the cards were destroyed.

Sears credit card	32.00	326.20
J.C. Penney's credit card	35.00	381.06
Local store credit card	42.36	444.91

The decision was to consolidate these bills totals into one loan, then destroy the cards.

Student loan	115.88	1,234.68
MasterCard	65.00	724.84
Mike's VISA card	85.00	1,255.00
Suzie's VISA card	97.60	2,524.07

These properties were deemed to be pleasure-deficient at this point in Mike and Suzie's life and were thus sold.

Ranch Club	257.00	16,859.00
Boat loan	136.40	5,019.22

Mike's check writing went from forty-three before his work, to twelve over the course of less than two months, then to an average of eight after five months. He no longer spent hours over his checkbook. Even better, he no longer spent days procrastinating over the process of paying the house bills.

WORKSHEET

Go through your checkbook ledger for the last three months to control your own check writing monster.

List checks for daily living that could have been paid for in cash:

_____

_____

_____

List pleasure-deficient possessions for which you are still making payments:

_____

_____

_____

List checks that are paying for credit:

_____

_____

_____

Decide what to do to eliminate checks made to credit companies:

Companies to be paid off:
By first month

_____   _____

_____   _____

By third month

_____   _____

_____   _____

By sixth month

_____   _____

_____   _____

By ninth month

_____   _____

_____   _____

By end of one year

_____   _____

_____   _____

Credit companies to be consolidated into one payment by a loan:

_____   _____

_____   _____

List of bills that continue to need to be covered by checks:

_____   _____

_____   _____

SESSION 6

The Secret to Life

I get these strange feelings of parental responsibility as a psychologist, as if my patients were my children and I am somewhat responsible for the way they think and feel. As I gain experience I try to talk myself out of these feelings, but they're always there in the back of my mind. Frequently, I question whether I am doing harm when my patient gets in a confused state, or gets upset by the therapy. I have to be confident in the process, and keep reminding myself that it works. No change is easy.

Mike came in very upset. Staring, glassy-eyed, lost in some cavernous mind cycle that shuts out the light of the world. My first thought was, "What did I do? Did I somehow hurt my own child? Take him too fast?" No joking today, no headfirst. Mike was hurt.

"Are you OK, Mike?"

He was dazed. On the verge of tears. He couldn't talk. He wanted to be hugged by his father, but men don't do that. He was feeling very alone. I moved and sat at my table right in front of him, inches away. I reached out and grabbed his forearm, squeezing. Reassuring.

"Mike, what happened to who?"
"Doc, I'm so damned confused. Life isn't supposed to be this way."
"Try to tell me what happened."
"It's Carol."

Mike started to cry a little. Then he got up from his seat cursing the fact that he was crying. A lot of guys have to get mobile when they cry in front of another man. Almost like they are walking away from it somehow.

"Did something happen to your girlfriend or did the two of you break up?"

"We broke up."

Mike is trying hard to fight the tears.

"I get all teary when relationships break up, too. Whose idea?"

"It was sort of mutual. She said we had to talk and I knew what she was going to say so I just made it easier for us and told her I didn't want to see her anymore. It's the best thing, I know. She was pretty upset, but it's the best thing."

"Did you ask her if that's what she wanted?"

"Well, she said she wanted to see other people, and . . ."

Mike just paused mid-sentence. Pauses like this often mean the person is filtering what they are going to say, re-creating the experience to cover something up. If you listen to people long enough, their filtering becomes very obvious. It is important as a psychologist, as another human being, not to judge someone who's filtering. Filtering is normal and not in the same category as deliberate lying. It's also easier to break down.

"Mike, it's me. You don't have to avoid telling me anything; I'm not judging you. In fact, I'll judge you less than you'll judge yourself. What is really going on?"

"I don't know. I've been feeling like I wanted to break up with Carol for awhile. I guess, I just saw my chance. What the hell is wrong with me? I've felt weird the last four or five weeks."

"Do have any idea what made you want to break up with Carol? What were you feeling when you were with her?"

"I was always aware that I was doing something wrong for the last few weeks. It kept getting stronger and stronger. I mean, I knew it was wrong before, but I could ignore it. It would never enter my mind. But recently, I don't know, I felt different."

"You do realize that you started therapy about six weeks ago?"

"Yeah, but we never talked about Carol. She never entered the conversation except maybe the first session. I feel sort of relieved, like a weight has been lifted. But I feel guilty about feeling relieved. And on top of that, I really miss her. It's so screwed up. What's going on?"

"I can't tell you for sure, but I'll give you a theory, if you want."

"Shoot."

"You start coming to therapy, to keep your head from exploding, as you said. You work for a number of weeks on simplifying the things in your life. In the process of working on simplifying, you recognize that the affair is a complicating thing. At the same time, you were finding an inner peace that wasn't consistent with being a man that was having an affair. That wasn't who you wanted to be. So it wore on your mind until you did something about it, until you purged that affair 'thing' from your life. You're relieved because you know that by reducing unnecessary things you will feel better. Guilty because the affair was like a 'thing' to you, like a possession that became pleasure-deficient."

Mike sat there open-mouthed trying to absorb what I was saying. I knew exactly what he was going to say next. Affairs and ending up in a psychologist's office with problems seem to occur together a lot.

"It makes sense except that Carol was not a thing to me. She was not like a possession. I actually ..."

"... loved her." *I couldn't resist finishing his sentence for him.* "You may have loved her after awhile, but Mike, it didn't start that way. She was a vehicle of fun, a diversion from your mundane life. She started as a 'thing.' That sounds terrible, but remember flirting, the pickup, the first night, the guys telling you to go for it. It's like that old Elvin Bishop song, 'Fooled Around and Fell in Love.' "

"Funny you should mention that song. I used to sing it to Carol all the time. Ah shit, if my affair was just a 'thing,' it is surely the hardest 'thing' to give up. But what if it is not a 'thing'? What if she's the girl who could make me happy the rest of my life? What if I just lost my last chance for real happiness?"

"Mike, let me ask you a question. If you were on the road and pulled over a guy for speeding, went up to his window, and he looked out and said, 'I had to go fast, the guy behind me was tailgating,' what would you say?"

"I'd pretend I was getting angry and I'd say to him: 'Mister, who's driving your car, you or the guy behind you?' "

"Well, who's driving *your* car, Mike? Whether you're happy or not has nothing to do with what the guy is doing in the car behind you. It's in your own car, inside of you. No one can make you happy unless you let them drive your car. Happiness and love all come from your own car. Don't look to other people to create positive feelings in you out of nowhere."

This is a hard concept for most of my patients to absorb. Many argue for weeks over the idea. I usually repeat it numerous times in therapy, because it is so important for us to understand. There are people with every-thing who are miserable and people with little who are happy. There are peo-ple in relationships who are treated well and are miserable, and people in relationships who are treated poorly and stay happy most of the day. It's inside, not outside. When we change the inside we will change our level of happiness. Then we may shape our outside to make maintaining happiness easier.

"Doc, I don't always agree with you at first. Actually, I rarely agree with you at first, but what you say makes sense later. If I can't find hap-piness through someone else, how do I find happiness? I'm not where I wanted to be right now."

"Mike, where were you going with your life a few years ago? How were you planning on making yourself happy back then? Where did you figure you'd be?"

"I didn't really know where I wanted to be back then."

"Then you made it!"

Mike chuckles. "You always make me laugh. Pointed sarcasm. So what you must be trying to tell me is that unless I set some goals, I'll never have a path to happiness. Not to say I won't have fun, 'cause I've had fun on many occasions. But happiness is different from fun, unless my goal is to have as much fun as possible. Right now, I'm not sure that's a good goal for me."

Silence. I was drifting into my own life.

"Did I say something wrong, Doc?"

"No, Mike. You're just making me think. You put that very well. I guess I've always been a goal-oriented person and maybe missed the fun part a little. You're right though, you need a balance. And for some people, having more fun is a good goal. Maybe not you, you've done the fun part well, but for a goal-oriented person fun can be a good goal."

"Doc, should I be charging you for this session?"

"Nope. I'm back. Did you see the movie "City Slickers"?

"Yeah."

"Remember the part where the city guy asks the cowboy what the secret to life is?"

"Yeah, I loved that. The Jack Palance character turns to Billy Crystal and puts up one finger and says, 'One thing, the secret to life is one thing.' Crystal asks what that one thing is and Palance says 'that's what you have to figure out.' "

"Good memory. That must have really meant something to you."

"Yeah, Doc, I think every man who has felt lost was waiting for Palance to answer that question. So Doc, what's the one thing?"

"Well, to Jerry Lewis it was raising money for muscular dystrophy, to Danny Thomas was St. Jude's Hospital. Ex-President Jimmy Carter builds homes for the poor in Georgia. Boxers want to win a title, writers want to publish a book. You don't always have to make it, but you can be happy trying."

"What's yours, Doc?"

"I want to shrink your head really small, Mike. Just kidding. I don't really have just one thing, I have a group of goals that I work on a couple at a time. I made a 'wish list' about twelve years ago of things I wanted to do or accomplish in my lifetime. I add to it all the time. It's got over a hundred items on it, and I've done about half."

"I've heard about that before."

"I read about it in a motivational book years ago, but a lot of successful people have talked about their wish lists."

"I know you're going to ask me to make up a wish list. Just answer this: If I'm trying to simplify the things in my life, doesn't putting a bunch of things down that I want sort of complicate life again?"

"It's not just things you put down, but experiences, accomplishments, goals. Don't think of goals in terms of owning a super sports car or the Vanderbilt mansion or something. Think of goals as experience you might want. For example, a goal might be to go sailing if you've never sailed before. That's very different from owning a sailboat. Put down experiences, places you might want to see, a charity you may wish to help. As we look at it, we might find your 'one or two secrets' for now. In fact, let's do 25 items together and you'll do 25 at home."

"I know the first experience I want on the list: I wish I'd prove my shrink completely wrong once."

"That's good, Mike. Maybe the second one could be even more realistic, like a trip to Mars or something."

EXERCISES

Mike and I spent the rest of the session putting a short wish list together. I've enclosed a copy of what we did at the end of the exercise. The exercise which follows focuses on the issues of this chapter.

Step 1: Get Out Your Address Book

Prior to making your wish list, I want you to take your address book and go through the names one by one. Make a list of the people that you have lost touch with or only talk to once a year or less. Make a second list of people you wish you knew better. Then make a third list of people in the book who serve a purpose in your life that perhaps has made them become more like a 'thing' rather than a relationship, Be honest with yourself. Remember, things serve purposes in three categories—necessities, status, and fun. If people on your list are there more for status than a relationship, put them on your list. For example, if you only remain friends with a local politician because he has a 'position,' put him down. If you only know your accountant because he does your taxes, put him down. It's not wrong to know someone just because he or she serves a purpose.

Step 2: Construct Your Wish List

Now you can begin constructing your own wish list. To begin, break it down into a few categories. Using your address book lists above, write down on your wish list worksheet the names of people with whom you would like to improve or change your current relationship.

Step 3: Set Your Priorities

List any causes or charities that you might want to participate in. You can also list any kinds of work you may wish to do, like distributing toys to needy children at Christmas.

Step 4: Choose Your Dreams

List any experiences you would like to have during the rest of your life. Let your imagination run wild. Wish list items do not always have to be easily attainable. You are not expected to have every experience that you list on your wish list. Try not to tie the experience to any particular person or place.

Step 5: Think About Traveling

List places you would like to visit in your lifetime. Remember, they do not have to be easily attainable, and you do not necessarily have to achieve all of them.

Step 6: Decide on Life Goals

List some of the goals you wish to accomplish during the rest of your life. Try not to tie them to individual people, but make them general goals.

Step 7: Make a Master List

When your worksheet is completely constructed, put it together into one wish list. Try to list as many items as possible, and add to the list whenever you want. For right now, pick one or two items on the list that might be attainable during the next year and begin to think about how you could make them happen in your lifetime. Refer to your list on a monthly basis.

WISH LIST WORKSHEET

Step 1
Lists of People

       A. People you have lost touch with
       B. People you wish you knew better
       C. People who you know but only to serve a purpose

Step 2
Begin Construction of Wish List

From the list above, write down the names of five or ten people with whom you would like to improve or change your current relationship

_____   _____   _____

_____   _____   _____

_____   _____   _____

Step 3
List any causes or charities with which you would like to be a partici-
pating member

_____   _____   _____
_____   _____   _____
_____   _____   _____

Step 4
List any experiences you would like to have at some point in your life

_____   _____   _____
_____   _____   _____
_____   _____   _____

Step 5
List any places you would like to visit in your life

_____   _____   _____
_____   _____   _____
_____   _____   _____

Step 6
List any goals that you have right now that you'd like to accomplish in
your life

_____   _____   _____
_____   _____   _____
_____   _____   _____

Step 7
Consolidate all the material into one overall wish list

_____   _____   _____
_____   _____   _____
_____   _____   _____

MIKE'S WISH LIST

1. Improve relationship with my wife
2. Improve relationship with daughter
3. Get reacquainted with Steve, Joe, and Bobby (high school friends)
4. Get to know new brother-in-law on a more social basis
5. Get involved in the Police Athletic League
6. Get involved with D.A.R.E. (Drug Abuse Resistance Education Program)
7. Get involved with police peer team to help other cops
8. Get involved again with church
9. Go whitewater rafting
10. Try windsurfing
11. Scuba dive in Caribbean
12. Run a 5K or 10K marathon
13. Solo in a plane
14. Go to Venice, Italy
15. Go to DisneyWorld with the boys
16. Backpack in Alaska
17. See the Aztec ruins
18. Get kids through college
19. Be more comfortable with myself
20. Set up a comfortable retirement
21. Publish an article in a police magazine

SUMMARY OF SIMPLIFYING THINGS

Five Steps:

1. Reduce your mental dependence on things.
2. Reduce the clutter in your life.
3. Concentrate on the importance of time rather than money or possessions.
4. Reduce the check writing and control the flow of money.
5. Look for direction from relationships, activities, and experiences you want rather than the ownership of more things.

SESSION 7

Look Out, Your Head
Is About to Explode

When we think of the hazards of being a cop, most people consider the potential physical dangers of the job. We consider the stress put on them by having to make life-threatening, split-second decisions. People even consider the turmoil of working around-the-clock shifts that can wreak havoc on their lives. What most people don't consider is the way these stresses can affect a person's personality, producing unhealthy changes in that way that person thinks and feels.

A study conducted with police recruits showed that by the time recruits had gone through the academy—never having even worked a day on the job—they became more cynical, authoritarian, and communicated less with non-cops. This doesn't just happen to policemen. It can happen to nurses, doctors, lawyers, business people, salespeople, and waiters and waitresses—all whose jobs shape a certain viewpoint about others and the world in general. Your job can add unhealthy tendencies to your personality. You need to be aware of these tendencies so that you can work to overcome them.

Mike came to the session in uniform, looking like he'd just been through a war.

"I hate lawyers. Shakespeare had the right idea when he said, 'First, kill all the lawyers.'"

"Nice to see you too, Mike. Actually, Shakespeare said that in reference to what would need to be done to create anarchy. It was actually a positive statement about lawyers."

"Yeah, well, killing all the lawyers is probably the most positive thing I could say about them, too."

"Don't break into lawyer jokes, Mike. They're just doing their jobs. Did you just testify today?"

"Yeah, how did you know?"

"After twelve years of working with cops, you just sort of sense these things. Maybe it's ESP; maybe you gave me a little subliminal hint. Who knows? What happened in court?"

"Well, it was one of those stupid cases. I get called to a domestic argument by one of the neighbors. It's one of those houses where there always seems to be fighting and calls are always coming in. I walk in with another of the guys who's retired now, and the husband is beating his wife and two children. He's drunk. We try to calm him down, but he keeps breaking free and smacking his wife or one of the kids. This goes on for half an hour, finally we tell him we're going to arrest him if he does it again. Naturally, he does. So we arrest him. It goes to court. The wife won't talk. The child protective worker stumbles over her notes, plus she never saw the abuse. And the defense lawyer treats me like I'm the criminal. He asks me questions such as, have I ever spanked my child, did I ever drink, wasn't I working a double that night. I mean, the guy is a known child abuser, and he's going to walk. It's just not right. It's not fair. I want to shoot the sonofabitch."

"What else is getting to you about this case?"

"Well, the retired guy moved to Florida, but could have come back and testified. The county would have paid for it. It would have made the case stronger. This abusive guy makes a shitload of money running a fake loan company that takes administration fees from poor farmers to find them loans, then never finds them anything. And, here I am trying to do the right thing in life and I get treated like a criminal."

"You're on a roll. What else is getting to you lately?"

"Ah, the school is screwing around with my kid. I just want a little extra reading help and they won't give it, so I was fighting with them yesterday."

"And ..."

"And, my wife's been on my case lately. She's upset, so I have to jump through hoops. That's not fair."

"And ..."

"And, they're talking about changing the shift schedule at work, so I'll probably get screwed by that. Nobody's doing what they're supposed to be doing."

"And ..."

"God, Doc, isn't that enough?"

"So how's your golf game?"

"That sucks too."

Mike and I simultaneously started to laugh. I find that if you can get the patient laughing when he's in that "all-is-wrong-with-the-world" mode you can start helping him put things into perspective.

"You know, Doc, since I've started coming here I sometimes sit up late at night thinking about how I've made such a mess of my life. I mean, I feel more focused now. You've been a big help so far, but I can't stop thinking about all the wrong decisions I've made, how I could be in a much better position in life than I am right now."

"Let me remind you, Michael, you weren't sleeping real well when you came in."

"Yeah, I guess that's true."

"Mike, do you know who Jonas Salk is?"

"Yeah, the polio vaccine guy."

"What if Jonas Salk said to you that all he could think about was the people who died while he was developing the vaccine? I mean, I'm sure there was a time when the vaccine was real close to being developed, but his research team just couldn't take that last step. What if Dr. Salk came up to you and said, 'Mike, I'm real depressed because of all those people I could have saved had I just developed this vaccine five years earlier.' What would you say?"

"I'd say that was ridiculous. I'd tell him not to be a jerk, that he'd done more for mankind than any hundred men, that he did more for medical science. And now you're going to tell me not to be a jerk, right?"

"Mike, I'm going to tell you to cut your losses."

"What do you mean? I'm not talking about money."

"Remember when we talked about that property a couple of sessions ago, and I said to cut your losses? Well, it's the same thing, except now it's time to cut your *emotional* losses."

"Thanks for reminding me, that property was another of my stupid decisions."

"OK, so you lost some money. But, don't cut your losses at just the money. If you spend time thinking about it and fretting over it, you just compound your financial losses into time losses."

"And time is life's most valuable asset. I thought I'd say that before you did."

"Leave the losses at just financial. Don't let other losses build up. Don't waste another minute of your life building on a mistake you already made—the same goes for the other bad decisions. Cut your losses!"

"OK, that makes sense. But it's easier said than done. How do I cut my losses?"

"Reduce your thinking. Did I ever tell you the pancake story?"

"Oh no, sounds like another one of those stupid jokes with a morale at the end."

"There is an old joke about a man who goes to see a psychologist. He says his wife made him go to therapy because he likes to eat pancakes for breakfast every morning. The psychologist laughs and replies that eating pancakes daily doesn't make a person mentally ill. In fact, the psychologist confesses he likes pancakes also. The man looks at the psychologist and says, 'You like pancakes too, Doc? Well, you should come over to my house, I have a whole attic full of them.' "

Mike manages a little chuckle.

"It wasn't that bad. So, hit me with the point."

"No point, just a joke."

"Nah, I don't believe it; there's got to be a point."

"Nope, no point, just a joke. Why? What point do you see, Mike?"

"Well, maybe all these bad thoughts are like pancakes in the attic and they build up until our attics are full."

"That's not bad. Could I use that? Or maybe it's not the idea of liking pancakes that's bad, but the extremeness that creates the mental problem."

Mike is screaming. "Ahhh, Ahhh, I knew there was a point. I knew you would never just let a joke go. Actually, I like my interpretation better."

"Actually, I like them both. If we don't get rid of our extremely bad thoughts, they will build up in our attics until we are mentally ill. We'll call it the pancake theory of psychology."

"Freud would be proud, Doc. So, I guess you're telling me I'm building up pancakes in my attic?"

"With lots of gooey syrup. If you keep it up, your head will explode."

"So, what are my pancakes?"

"Well, pancakes come with the job. Extreme thinking that can just carry over, like 'right and wrong' thinking."

"Let me give this one a shot. On the job there are definite rights and wrongs. If a guy is robbing a bank, that's wrong. All I have to do is find the law against it and the decision is made. But in the outside world there aren't rights and wrongs, but a bunch of stuff in between. I'm used to right-and-wrong thinking, and that can cause problems in other parts of life."

"Pretty good for a street cop. When our work causes us to think one way, thinking can get real complicated when the world outside of work has different rules. The same is true of facts and opinions. Police work is a fact-based world—I saw x, y, and z. But the outside world is mostly opinion-based. That's why you had a hard time handling the court system, which is opinion-based. It is a fact that guy was beating his child; it is an opinion as to whether he was right or wrong. Extreme thinking—such as fact-based thinking or right-wrong thinking—complicates life. It is also a natural part of your job."

"What are some of the other extreme ideas I have to worry about?"

"There's fair and unfair. What's fair to the lion in the jungle isn't fair to the zebra he preys on. I mean, the zebra gets up one morning all happy, takes a break to rest, and he's dinner. Is that fair to the zebra? Then there's the idea of good and bad guys. Bad guys usually aren't all bad, and good guys usually aren't all good. There are many more examples. Generally, whenever you overgeneralize or exceed the bounds of reality, you set yourself up for an extreme idea."

"Exceeding the bounds of reality—that's a heavy idea in itself. I guess it's sort of like when we talked about what was really a 'need,' or not. You get cued into the thinking by the use of the word 'need.' "

"And other words can cue you into other extreme ideas. Words like 'should,' 'supposed to,' and 'have to' when referring to someone else's or your own behavior will cue you into an extreme thought. Words like 'awful,' 'terrible,' 'sucks,' and 'I can't stand it' cue you into other extreme thoughts. With the extreme thoughts come extreme feelings. Extreme feelings create desperation. While all this is going on, life is very complicated and we start to lose control."

"So, as with the word 'need,' if I become aware of the words behind my feeling and use less desperate words, the feeling will change. I think I've heard or read this somewhere else before."

"Mike, I don't come up with much new stuff. Most of this was around in the Greek and Roman days, or in the Bible or other religious books. Psychologists and psychiatrists have presented the ideas as if they're new, but we basically are just reworking old ideas so they make sense to people who are upset or want to lead better lives. Remember, Mike, the goal is to think simpler. Sometimes our media tries to paint extremes, but most of daily life is not extreme until we make it so. Unfortunately, a lot of your job is extreme, but a lot is mundane. I remember Sgt. Joe Friday on "Dragnet" saying that being a cop was 'hours and hours of boredom with moments of sheer terror.' A lot of life is that way. Sometimes the boredom is worse than the terror, so we elevate the boring times by exaggerating their significance, like you were doing 30 minutes ago. Most of that stuff is just daily life crap. Don't exaggerate it. Work it through, cut your emotional losses, and figure out what you're going to do to enjoy the rest of the day."

"Sometimes, I guess I don't want to think reasonably. That guy in court, even if they let him go he'll probably do something else and get himself back there. I did my job. It's not my job to prosecute him and punish him. If the court doesn't do its job, I can't help it. As for reading and the school, I know my wife and I are going to be the ones who end up helping our kid, and I guess that's not so bad. My wife will get off my case sooner or later, she always does. And I really don't know anything about that shift schedule so I should wait to pass judgment on that."

"What about your golf game?"

"Doc, I don't know what to do to figure out that damn game."

"Me either, Mike. I'm sure there's an answer to fixing my game, but I have no idea what it is. I do know one thing though, the answer will be simple."

EXERCISES

It is important to understand the way thoughts control emotions. Many people do not want to accept this notion because it suggests that they can have complete control over their emotions. People like to think of thoughts and emotions are automatic. If a bad situation happens, they just believe that the situation causes them to feel and think certain ways. As long as people believe that way, their lives will continue to be complicated. It is, however, not easy to control either emotions or thought. It will take an extraordinary amount of persistence.

The basic technique to controlling thought and feeling is to confront the extremeness of the words you use to talk both to yourself and to others. It is not necessary to actually say these words of extremeness out loud; even if you think them you will be overcomplicating your life. A general rule is that if you feel badly, then somewhere in your self-talk there are some of these words of extremeness. If you can discover what words and sentences you say to yourself and lessen the extremeness, you will start to control your own feelings. You will not be able to make an unpleasant situation pleasant, but you will certainly be able to lessen your unpleasant feelings. Generally, it is best to begin by changing these words out loud; later it will become automatic.

The major words, phrases, and concepts of extremeness follow. The exercises will help you to change them in your life. They are only a start; to completely absorb this concept you must practice it over a long period of time. Remove extremeness from your life, and complications will reduce. Remove extremeness, and you will have learned to cut your emotional losses.

Extreme words and phrases

awful	terrible	catastrophic
sucks	should	need
have to	suppose to	must
I can't stand it	can't take it	

Concepts that are relative—they are valid only in relation to a standard

fair and unfair	truth
good and bad	just and unjust
facts	

Less extreme words to be used instead

annoying: instead of awful, terrible, etc.
not as I would have liked: instead of awful, terrible
beneficial to do: instead of have to, supposed to, should
want: instead of need
difficult to accept: instead of I can't take it or stand it
would be better: instead of must, should

How to make relative terms valid

Fair and unfair, just and unjust: Statements of fairness must be viewed relative to the person toward which they are oriented. To say that something is fair from Mike's point of view, or even fair to the parties involved, is valid. To say something is unfair in nature is extreme. Even statements of valid fairness have a factor of opinion in them.

Truth: Truth is a completely relative term. Everyone perceives every situation differently. Therefore, everyone's truth is different. To state truth validly it must be noted whose point of view it reflects. "This is Mike's truth" is a valid statement. "Mike saw the real truth" is not valid; it is extreme and can lead to emotional difficulties.

Facts: What was said about truth applies to facts. Facts are only based upon someone's perceptions, or upon a standard in a fact-based system, as in Mike's case. To state that a criminal stole money from a bank is a fact when stealing money is defined as removing money from a bank without permission of the bank. If the case goes to court and it comes out that the money was his, one could hold the opinion that the money was not stolen, even though it fits the definition. People who work in fact-based systems should exercise care to not think that the non-work world is fact-based. Newspapers report opinions, not facts. Judges give opinions, not facts.

Good and bad: As facts, the notions of good and bad are based on a standard and a definition. What is good to one person may be bad to another. Whenever you use these terms, try to state the evaluation in terms of reaching a goal.

Exercise 1

Read the dialogue of my first session with Mike and recognize the times that he uses extreme words. Each time he does, ask yourself what feeling these extreme words created in him. With each use of these extreme terms try to change the wording to lessen the feeling for Mike.

Exercise 2

In the following sentences, see if you can change the wording from extreme words to non-extreme words. Mike's responses follow the exercises. Do them yourself before you look at Mike's responses:

You should go to the store today.
I can't stand when you act that way.
I need to have a new TV set.
It's not fair when the boss doesn't give me the raise I deserve.
Don't try to tell me you didn't talk badly about me. I know that's not the truth.
You must pay more attention to this proposal.
The way I have been treated is just terrible, awful. He's supposed to be nice to me.
Don't argue facts with me. I saw it with my own eyes.

Exercise 3

Think of a situation that made you very emotionally upset. Then do the following:
Describe the situation from your point of view.
Recognize the extreme thoughts that created your emotions in that situation.
Describe how the situation turned out.
Determine which words and sentences you could have used that would have lessened your emotions in that situation.

Exercise 4

Repeat Exercise 3 the next time you have an unpleasant situation.

MIKE'S RESPONSES TO EXERCISES

You should go to the store today.
It is a good idea to go to the store today. I think it would be to your advantage.

I can't stand when you act that way.
I do not like the way you are acting. Could you be more aware of this, please?

I need to have a new TV set.
I want a new TV set.

It's not fair when the boss doesn't give me the raise I deserve.
I think I deserve a raise, but it seems the boss doesn't agree. He has a

right to his opinion, and I have a right to mine. I don't like that we don't agree because I don't get the raise.

Don't try to tell me you didn't talk badly about me. I know that's not the truth.

I have heard that you have said bad things about me from a person that has always been reliable. If that's not what you believe happened then you might want to be aware that this is the way others are seeing it.

You must pay attention to this proposal.

This proposal is very important and it would seem to be in your best interest to pay attention to it. I would like you to look at it closely.

The way I have been treated is terrible, awful. He's supposed to be nice to me.

I do not like being treated the way I've been treated. It is not what I would have expected.

Don't argue facts with me. I saw it with my own eyes.

We seem to have seen the same situation in two different ways. Since I saw it with my own eyes, it doesn't make much sense to argue with me as I'm not likely to change my opinion.

SESSION 8

Mental Pinball: The Ultimate Head Game

Psychotherapy gets easier after the first seven or eight sessions. The patient is used to working, rapport—if it is going to happen—is well established, and usually there is a positive change in the patient's life. In fact, there are people who suggest that most, if not all, of the change a person is going to make happens in the first few sessions. Generally, most therapists will agree that while the greatest change happens at first, the stability of change depends on continued help and application of the principles to day-to-day life.

With a patient like Mike, therapy starts to get a little more freeform. In the first sessions, I almost always know what I'm going to try to get across. In the later sessions, I know what else we need to discuss, but I look for openings, rather than trying to determine session subjects up front. When people start talking about thoughts there is always an opening for one point or another.

"I've been telling everybody the pancake story. We now call you Dr. Pancakes around my house."

"Gee, it's great to be reduced to the punchline of a bad joke. How have you been this week, Mike?"

"It's amazing the difference a week can make."

"What do you mean?"

"It's funny, I was so negative last week and this week I don't really feel that bad at all. In fact, I sort of feel pretty good."

"I guess all your problems have been solved, and your golf game is on track."

"No, that's the best part. I still have the same problems, and I still can't hit a five iron, but I feel pretty good."

"That's great, Mike. So tell me about work during the last week."

"Now that's a real downer. My sergeant has been a real pain in the ass lately. He's been catching it about quotas and overtime, so he takes it out on us. He called me in and told me I was slacking off and that he was going to have to write a memo for my file if I didn't start writing more tickets. Then, a week later he calls me in and recommends me for a citation for my investigative work on a couple of recent collars. Here I am giving up investigative work to write tickets, and he gives me an honor for exactly what I was doing in the first place. Not to mention that investigation takes overtime, which he complains about all the time."

"Yeah, it really makes you wonder what it's all about. How about home, Mike? Did your wife get off your case?"

"Nah, she's just about the same. She complains if I work overtime, then complains I don't make enough money. She complains if I don't get the work done around the house, then complains if I don't spend more time with her and the kids. I feel like I'm always jumping through hoops for her. You know, sometimes life really ..."

"Whoa, Mike, hold up. Look what just happened here. You were in a great mood, then all of a sudden you're about to condemn the world."

"Yeah, Doc, thanks. You just have a way of making people feel good."

"I have a way! I haven't even gotten a chance to say anything. You're playing pinball."

"Pinball? What are you talking about?"

"You just played mental pinball with yourself. It's the ultimate head game. You were feeling good about life, then you started talking about how other people want you to act and how you changed to please them. Then they told you something else, and you changed again to please them. Then you're told something else, and you change again. It's pinball—you go from bumper to bumper, then bounce off the flippers a few times, trying to score enough points to get an extra ball or something."

"Then I get pissed off and go through the middle in a crash and burn."

"You got it. And it's all based on a couple simple myths of life."

"Here it comes."

"The myth that people are consistent, and the myth that we can somehow meet other people's expectations and make them happy."

Mike thinks for a long time on these ideas. There is always a strange look that comes over a patient's face when you tell him something he already knows, but acts in a way opposite to his own knowledge. These two ideas aren't new to Mike any more than they are to you. But, many times we just seem to expect the opposite of what we know. We expect to be able to constantly meet people's expectations and make them happy, and we expect other people to be consistent from day to day.

"I disagree in a way, I think."

"That sounds real sure. OK, Mike, shoot."

"Well, I can meet other people's expectations by doing things they tell me they want done, even though I know I don't 'drive their car' as you say."

"I'll agree, given certain conditions. Given that people will tell you everything they want done in life at any given moment, and the way they want it done, and how that might change when their mood changes, and how that might change when the state of the world changes or something new happens to them."

"I see the point on that one. There's too many variables to get into someone's head, therefore you can never expect to meet what they want. But people are consistent in some ways, some times."

"Come on, Mike. Consistent some ways, some times. Don't they call that an oxymoron, saying contradictory statements in one phrase?"

"It must be terrible, always being right."

"I'm not always right. That lobotomy thing I had a few years ago slowed me up a lot."

"Very funny. Let's see, if people aren't consistent, and I can't expect to meet people's expectations, where does that leave me?"

"Simple. You're a person trying to do the best you can and be happy."

"There's that word again. Simple. But people always have expectations of you and you can't help that. Like, what am I supposed to do at work when the guy comes up to me and says I'm not doing my job because I'm not writing enough tickets, and I'm doing too much overtime? I mean, I have to defend myself."

"Are you doing something wrong given your available knowledge at the time?"

"No, I would just do investigations instead."

"Then what do you have to defend yourself from?"

"I'm being accused."

"If someone comes into the precinct accused of a crime, what's usually the first indication he's guilty?"

"He has a ton of reasons why he didn't do it. So you're saying I act like I'm guilty?"

"Even when you're not. The minute you become defensive, you seem guilty. The minute you provide an excuse, you look guilty. It's like the guy running from the crime scene. You gotta chase after him."

"It makes sense, but what do I do instead?"

"State that you are working hard in other areas and if they want a change, let them know that they have to make that decision. Leave it up to them. Or if it's an area you disagree on, try to leave it a mutual disagreement, a difference of opinion."

"That sounds good, but try to do that in the police department and you'll get your head handed to you."

"Prove it to me."

"What?"

"Prove it to me, Mike. Hand me my head. I'll be you, you be your sergeant."

"You're in trouble. I'm good at these role plays."

"Give it to me then."

"OK, here goes, Doc. Get your butt in my office right now!"

Mike was really going to get into this.

"Sure, Sergeant."

"Don't give me any of your lip. I'm not in the mood."

He was trying to trap me, so I didn't respond.

"Officer, you have one of the lowest levels of writing tickets in the precinct."

Statement of fact. No response necessary.

"That is completely unsatisfactory. If you don't straighten up, I'm going to put you on report. Don't you have anything to say for yourself?"

"I hear you saying that you want me to change my focus away from the investigative work I've been doing to writing more tickets. It's a shift of focus. I can handle that change."

"Your work production has been very poor, officer."

"I can see that you are very upset with my work, and I think I need a little guidance at this point. What I'd like to do, sergeant, is sit down with you and show you what I've been doing lately and maybe you could show me where you'd like me to change my time usage from this point on. I can't change what I did at this point, even though I thought I was doing good work. We could discuss what amount of time should be used on patrol and what amount on investigation, and other things."

"You know how to do your job. Just do it."

"I feel your goals on my time usage are different from mine. Please, meet with me so we can go over scheduling."

"You've been on the job long enough to know what you are supposed to do."

"Sergeant, I know I've been working hard, but probably in a different direction, and I just want to make sure we are on the same page."

Mike decides to end the role playing.

"That's enough, Doc. He'd probably throw me out of his office by now and tell me to forget it. You never defended yourself, did you? How did you do that?"

"Defending oneself is very complicated and seldom works anyway. If you are simply doing what you think you are supposed to, you're not guilty of anything, and if you understand the myths of expectations, you can respond without defending yourself. Just don't be suckered into defending yourself. Focus on what you can change, not what he didn't like about your performance."

"But Doc, if I change at this point to please him, isn't that just pinballing again?"

"It's not pinballing when you leave the decision up to him. Pinballing is when you get a lot of demands and try to meet them all, making your own assumptions of what you can best do to please someone else. For example, you said your wife will make five demands on you and expect them all to be done simultaneously. If you try to assume what to do and defend yourself when she is not happy you will pinball. If you tell her you can do one and leave it up to her, then you are not pinballing. If she changes and is not happy, that's not your problem. Understand the myths."

" 'Understand the myths.' Do you mean that people are not consistent, and I can't expect myself to constantly meet others' expectations?"

"Correct. If you keep this in mind then no one will be able to pinball you. Don't take their attack as an attack, see it as a means to open a conversation about goals and time. Most attacks come from misinformation."

"What do you mean?"

"Most attacks come because people don't understand others' motives. Let's see, how do I get this across? Have you ever been in a situation where you seemed like the bad guy when you were trying to do something good?"

This, by the way, is a stupid question to a cop. Anyone who has been "on the job" more than a couple of days has had their intentions misinterpreted. Cops are seen by many people as being bad guys when they are trying to do good. Actually, it's probably a stupid question to anyone. We all are misinterpreted at various points in our lives. However, stupid questions aren't always bad if they elicit the information you want.

"Ever been in a situation! That's a laugh. I remember one time I was patrolling at the bus station with my partner. There was this drunk guy bothering people on the platform. We tried to get him to move along, but he wouldn't. So we were going to put him in the car and move him away from the area; we weren't even going to arrest him. Well, we started to walk with him to the car and he pulls out my partner's gun. We jump him to get the gun away. We're wrestling with him on the ground, but he won't give up the gun. He's really strong. I put my chest in front of the barrel because I have a vest on and I want to make sure if he shoots no one gets hurt, the vest will just absorb it. I was proud of my bravery. Meanwhile, the guy's screaming bloody murder. During the tussle, a bus pulls in and the people getting out see this whole fiasco. They start yelling at my partner and me for brutality and throw stuff at us all the way back to the car. I remember thinking, 'What the hell am I doing this for? I should have let him shoot one of them.' People are really assholes sometimes. I guess that's a decent example of being misinterpreted."

Mike gets a little choked up as he tells this story. I only wish it was an isolated story, but I've heard hundreds just like it. There seems to be a general trend in our society to assume people are guilty before they are proved to be so. Law enforcement officers, particularly, are often thought of as guilty of misconduct whenever the situation is close. I hope this trend turns around—it makes life complicated. No wonder cops tend to score high on scales of cynicism.

"Yeah, Mike, that was a good example. See the power of misinformation? This story affects you even to this day. If they had the right information, they wouldn't be accusing you of brutality. If they knew motive, they wouldn't attack. If you start seeing communications as misinformation rather than attacks, you'll deal with them more effectively. Don't be those people getting off the bus! Find out the story first. That's all I did when you were playing your sergeant. Find out the story and solve the problem."

"Let me use your own words, Doc. If I stop defending myself, try my hardest and treat attacks as misinformation, I will focus my responses to people based on what can happen in the future rather than what went wrong in the past. I will stop looking guilty in these situations. By focusing on what will happen, I will make my responses and my life simpler."

"You are amazing. You even got the concept of simplicity in there. You might just make it, Mike. Life is always simpler when you focus on the future when in conflict. It's always simpler when you recognize the limits of human existence, such as that people are not consistent and you can't meet everyone's expectations. It's always simpler when you don't respond to everything as an attack."

"I think I've got it. Mental pinball—bouncing off other people's expectations and attacks—is like being a pinball bouncing off bumpers. You know, I don't always defend myself."

"I figured that in your incident at the bus depot you wanted to rebel rather than defend yourself."

"Yeah, that's what I tend to do with my wife. When I get pissed off enough, I rebel. I don't do anything when she wants me to do something; sometimes I even counterattack. I think I just keep digging myself into a deeper and deeper hole when I rebel."

"That's what usually happens when you rebel. And the hole gets deep real quick, with all kinds of negative emotions piled on it. In many ways, rebellion is worse than defending yourself."

"On top of that, when you rebel you feel bad about it later. You feel like an ungrateful teenager. Anyway, I brought that up so you'd know

that I don't always just defend myself. I get worse sometimes."
    "I guess you're not consistent either, huh, Mike?"

EXERCISES

It is inevitable that people will be accused of doing something wrong many times in their lives. The times we become most emotional about these accusations are when we believe that we have been doing what we were supposed to do and are being falsely accused. When this occurs we have to fight our natural tendency to fight back or defend ourselves. Life becomes very complicated when it is spent engaging in either justification or defense. Remember, it takes two people to have an argument. If you do not argue or defend, the fight is over. Understanding that we can't always meet others' expectations because people are not *consistent* in their expectations will guide us in responding to accusation. The exercises which follow are designed to help you learn the thought process. Mike's responses can be found at the end of the exercises. In a later chapter, you will revisit the ideas of future orientation and solving problems in confrontational situations.

Exercise 1

Describe a situation in your life where your positive intentions were misinterpreted. In your description, try to write not only your point of view, but what you think the other person must have seen to believe that your actions stemmed from bad intentions. After you have described the situation, look closely at how you handled it in an effort to clear up the misinterpretation. Was there any defensiveness on your part, or any rebellion? Picture a more productive way you could have handled it. Be careful. Looking back at better ways of handling a situation is only designed to teach you; do not degrade yourself for your perceived mistakes. Remember to keep a future orientation even when looking back.

Exercise 2

Describe a situation in which you were responded to defensively. Look at your own actions to see if you may have misinterpreted intention rather than dealt with just the actions of the other person. From your position, how could you have handled a defensive response? Also, for extra practice, decide how the sergeant could have better handled Mike as described in this chapter.

Exercise 3

List five current expectations for each of the following people in your life:

Spouse, boyfriend, girlfried, or significant other
1. _____   2. _____   3. _____
4. _____   5. _____

Child
1. _____
2. _____
3. _____
4. _____
5. _____

Closest friend
1. _____
2. _____
3. _____
4. _____
5. _____

Parent
1. _____
2. _____
3. _____
4. _____
5. _____

Boss
1. _____
2. _____
3. _____
4. _____
5. _____

Exercise 4

For each of those people above, list an expectation that has changed in the past couple of years, or an expectation that has been added. Be aware of the inconsistency of expectations.

Spouse, boyfriend, girlfriend, or significant other
1. _____   2. _____   3. _____
4. _____   5. _____

Child _____

Closest friend _____

Parent _____

Boss _____

Exercise 5

Describe a time in your life when you have pinballed. Remember, pinballing is trying to make a lot of people happy, bouncing from expectation to expectation. Be aware that the best way to stop pinballing is to decide to do what you feel is best, or come to a decision and do not defend your actions. Focus any further conversations on what will be done *next* rather than what has been done that didn't make someone happy. If you keep your conversations future-focused, they will be simpler.

MIKE'S RESPONSES TO EXERCISES

Exercise 1

I had sent Suzie flowers one day from work early in the morning because we had been getting along very well. At the end of the shift, I had a late arrest and ended up being forced to do overtime. When I had gotten home, Suzie was "freaking out," accusing me of sending her flowers so that I could go out drinking with the boys and come home late. In the first place, the two were not connected because I sent the flowers long before I knew I would be staying late. Secondly, I was at work with an arrest, not out with the boys. When she started the fight, I got angry and told her I wasn't going to try anymore. I rebelled. Then I went out to the place where everyone hangs out. I guess it would have been best not to leave and not to defend myself because I looked guilty when I did both of these. If I would have calmly held my ground, she probably would have come around in about an hour or so.

Exercise 2

I confronted my sergeant on why I was turned down for a transfer to a more prestigious unit after he told me I would probably get it. I thought I knew the answer which was that someone had an "in" and I was passed over to make room for somebody who had "kissed ass." The sergeant got real defensive. I would have handled it better by hearing his explanation first, then making plans for how to make the transfer later. Instead he got angry at me and the whole idea of my transfer got dropped.

Exercise 3

Expectations

Suzie
keep the kids quiet when I am sleeping during the day when I've worked the night shift
keep the kids happy and taken care of
keep the social calendar for the family
not get me involved in things I don't want to do
be a good wife and mother

Children
keep quiet when I am sleeping during the day after midnight shifts
do well in school
don't talk back
be appreciative
come to us when there are problems

Closest friend
be there for me when I need him
stand behind me if I get in trouble
don't tell other people what I tell him
don't be too nosy
be there to have fun with

Parent
don't be too much of a burden
tell me when they need help
be a good grandparent to my kids

be there on holidays
be there for support when needed

Boss
don't give mixed messages
make sure I get what I deserve when I do well
be kind when correcting me
be honest
give me help when I need it

Exercise 4
Changed expectations

Spouse
Changed expectation about doing all the housework. I pitch in more.

Child
Changed expectation of daughter to call occasionally and let me know how she is doing.

Closest Friend
Added expectation that he shouldn't be too nosy about my home life.

Parent
Changed expectation of how much work I will have to do to take care of them.

Boss
Changed expectation of how willing he is to help my career.

Exercise 5
Since I pinball all the time, this one is easy. When my daughter was a teen and I was meeting Suzie, I kept expecting to please both of them all the time. My daughter hated Suzie and would constantly say bad things about her. I would defend Suzie to my daughter, then confront Suzie with what was being said. I was constantly arguing with both of them to get along better, but by my actions I wasn't helping the situation because I was remaining in between. Finally, it ended up with nobody getting along. I would have done better to stay out of the middle and keep oriented toward the future when they would get along. Now they the are best of friends, and I'm on shaky ground with both of them.

SESSION 9

If It Was a Snake, You'd Have Fang Marks on Your Nose

I have a strange memory of Mike's next session. Not because of what took place, that was ordinary, but because of my own foul mood. I was having a bad day. I couldn't stop thinking about happenings in my own life. Obsessiveness is a characteristic found in many doctors of all disciplines. I guess the process of getting into graduate schools and getting through it all tends to select out people that both work and think real hard. It was a day when I least wanted to be listening to other people. It was one of "those days."

It was the last appointment of the day, after eleven hours of hearing people's troubles. When I saw that Mike was next in my appointment book I remember I was happy. He was an easier patient at this point. He wasn't in crisis anymore. I didn't anticipate I'd have to focus intently on every word he was saying. I could relax a little. Time goes faster when you're not always trying to stop the bleeding. I had one of those banana smiles when I greeted Mike. He looked at my big smile and said:

"Doc, are we really doing what we need to be doing here?"

Suddenly, I wasn't sure I liked him anymore. Therapeutic doubt. I wasn't in the mood for that kind of hard work. I have problems too. My mind was full. Now I have to prove myself to him.

"Nice to see you too, Mike. Perhaps we could engage in a little small talk before we destroy the entire process of psychotherapy."

"Sorry, Doc. How are you?"

How am I? I've been here for twelve hours without even a break to go to the bathroom, much less eat lunch. Everybody is calling with a crisis. I can't stop thinking about my own problems, and now I get to listen to you complain. How should I be? I'd rather be home, or driving in my car listening to music, or in the Bahamas sipping piña coladas (and I'm allergic to coconut). Besides, you don't really care how I am. You have something on your mind and wouldn't even have asked if I wasn't sarcastic a few minutes ago. You were supposed to be easy today. What the hell happened?

"I'm fine, Mike, just fine. Thanks for asking. Now what is it that is bothering you so much?"

"I don't know. I just had one of those tremendous days of insight the last 24 hours, and I can't make sense of it all. I guess it's just upsetting me a little."

"Well, Mike, days of insight are quite common when you are in therapy. I mean, we've done a lot of work here and ..."

"Doc, don't take this wrong, but my insight has nothing to do with you. In fact, I'm not sure I'm getting what I need out of these sessions. I'm not sure you're doing this therapy right."

Now why is it that God seems to want to test my patience just at the time when I am least capable of measuring up? At this point, I just want to scream, jump up, and pound him silly. But life is choices. It would be unprofessional. It would be a bad business move. Besides, he's got a gun.

"You are full of surprises, Mike. I guess that's why I like you so much. Now how did I go from being a good therapist last week to 'yak dung' this week?"

"Touchy. Guess I didn't say that right. Let me tell you what's going on. Since I started therapy and making all these changes, my wife has been trying harder too. She doesn't want to come in just yet, so she's gone out and has been reading a lot of these psychology books. Well, two nights ago we started having these discussions about our lives and why we are the way we are and ..."

Oh no! I knew what was coming. Let me describe my office to you: I was sitting on a couch across the room from the door and he was on another couch on the perpendicular wall. My desk was across the room about 20 feet away, on the same wall as the door. When he started, all I could think about was this huge bottle of aspirin I had in my upper right desk drawer. Soon I was going to be wanting a couple real bad. I couldn't get up to get them. That would be too obvious. If I could get over to my desk on some pretense, I could sneak a few in the process. I'd just yawn, cover my mouth, then pop them in. But, I couldn't think of an excuse to go to the desk. So I sat there thinking about whether I could open the drawer and fly the aspirin over to me by some sort of mental telekinesis. If only I had been born with "My Favorite Martian's" finger, or Samantha's nose in "Bewitched.")

"... and, so she was describing to me that we both come from dysfunctional families, and how that determines the path of our whole lives. My father was an inattentive sort, cold and withdrawn a lot. My mother always acquiesced to him, leaving my feelings unresolved. This created such rage in me that I became a 'rage-aholic.' I tempered the rage with sports when I was younger, and became a cop so I could continue to rage and take out my anger on society in a socially acceptable fashion. Being addicted to the rage, I also fear it, and that makes me fear relationships because I don't want to lose control. This causes me to be 'commitmentphobic,' so relationships in my life don't work."

"Boy, hearing this, Mike, just makes me cringe."

"It gets worse! My wife comes from a dysfunctional family too! She has this handicapped sister and figured out that she grew up feeling guilty because she was the normal one and her problems were nothing compared to her sister's. She always put herself aside to take care of her sister and not be a burden on her parents. But her sister got all the attention, so she figured that she must be beneath her sister because she didn't get any attention. So she never developed any self-esteem, and that's why she ended up marrying someone with as many problems as I have and became 'co-dependent.'"

"Wow, all that and you're still expected to get up in the morning."

"Doc, I wonder how people can go through life and not realize these important things about themselves."

"So, Mike, what does all this great knowledge have to do with why therapy isn't working for you?"

"Well, we're just not dealing with the real issues. We're not attacking what's 'deep down inside' me, the real things that are bothering me, controlling me."

"Deep down inside." When I hear someone say "deep down inside" I feel like

beating them over the head with a pepperoni. Where is this "deep down inside"? Is there a hidden ventricle in the heart that medical science hasn't found yet? Is there a secret room somewhere in the body that isn't on the architectural sketches? Is there a place in that gray, gooey stuff on the outside of our brains that is marked "deep down inside"? Are we the only animals with a "deep down inside"? Do chickens have a "deep down inside," and what would it taste like in a garlic sauce?

"Mike, before this ... uh ... enlightenment, weren't you starting to feel a little better?"

"Yeah, actually I was feeling great. I thought I was starting to get it together. Little did I realize."

"Yeah, little did you realize. Excuse me, Mike. I need to go over to my desk and get a piece of paper."

"What do you need paper for?"

"Uh ..., let me see. I might want you to do this exercise. I'll show you later. Yyaahhhh, excuse me for the yawn, Mike, it's been a long day."

"Well, Doc, what do you think about what my wife and I figured out?"

"Pretty entertaining. You just missed a few points."

"Like what?"

"For starters you missed the toilet training cycles."

"What!?"

"Well, so much of life depends on your toilet training. You obviously were rewarded very heavily for going to the bathroom when you were being toilet trained. Rewarded way too much, so you learned that by expulsing something, you get a good feeling about yourself just like you did when toilet trained. That's why you spend so much and don't deny yourself anything."

"Really, I don't even remember toilet training."

"You don't have to remember. It's 'deep down inside.' You also have a real hard time sharing because you wanted to possess your mom too much. You wanted her to be your own, in more ways than just a mother. Dad was in the way, and you wanted to kill him. Your sister was competition, so you hate her."

"Are you sure? I love my sister."

"When I say hated your sister I actually meant you loved your sister. It's one of those mental-psychology-secret things. But you love her too much. You wish she wasn't your sister so you could be with her. That way, you could be with your mother at the same time, 'cause sis is like mom. You can't keep a relationship because of these urges for the women in your own family. It even goes back to your grandmother who was always loving. You want to be with her too, but that's really 'deep inside,' passed down through generations."

"You're really starting to piss me off. Who the hell do you think you are? I started to believe you for a second, but I think you're just messed up. I don't want any ..."

"Then again, maybe you're just a regular human being and I'm making all this up to piss you off."

Mike pauses.

"What's going on, Doc?"

"Take a deep breath. It's just you and me, Mike. Now, that toilet training stuff and wanting your mother was a bunch of older theories in psychology. I was trying to demonstrate what happens when you start analyzing everything. What was happening to you?"

"I was getting more and more upset."

"Upset and unsettled. What do you think the point is here, Mike?"

"When you analyze, you get upset?"

"Or unsettled."

"Which was exactly what I was doing thinking about what my wife and I discussed. So you're saying insight is bad for you? I thought psychologists believed in that stuff."

"Insight that leads to action or goal setting isn't bad, but if it just sits out there and makes you analyze it could hurt you. Plus, overanalysis can tend to stray from simplicity and the obvious."

"I knew the 'simple thing' was coming. What do you mean?"

"Let's look at why you became a cop. Your wife says it was so you could continue to rage, express anger, and control society. Do you remember your decision to become a cop?"

"Well, it wasn't a big decision. I was working as a carpenter occasionally. I wanted to go to school and be a lawyer or a reporter. I liked the idea of finding out stuff, investigating. I never thought about being a cop. Anyway, a couple of my friends were taking the police test, and I needed to change jobs, so I figured I'd take the test, too; I could always not take the job. When I was called I hadn't worked ten days the previous two months, so I figured I'd do it because it was steady and I could always quit when I finished school. There were other reasons about the work and stuff, but I don't quite remember those."

"Does that sound like rage, expressing anger, wanting control?"

"No, Doc."

"Or does it seem like you made a logical decision based on wanting to make your life better at the time?"

"It made sense then. I was improving my life."

"Rather than analyze, look to the simplest and most obvious answer first. In science it's called parsimony. Always accept the simplest explanation for an event. Parsimonious means stingy or frugal. Be stingy with how much leeway you will give beyond a simple interpretation."

I was aware at this point that my obsessions about my problems were coming from my own overanalysis. I was starting to feel better myself, my mind was clearing, which frequently happens when you do therapy.

"What about being a 'rage-aholic,' doc?"

"I wasn't even aware you were raging that much lately."

"No, actually I've been very calm for a long time. I don't really rage that much anyway."

"Why did she call you a rage-aholic?"

"She says when I don't rage, I'm just 'in remission,' whatever the hell that means."

"It means that a disease is still present, but its symptoms are not being shown at the present. Mike, we all have tendencies one way or another. You might have a tendency to get angry or rage, but it doesn't mean it is a disease. We choose to let our tendencies take over or not. Some might have a tendency to be shy or be overweight, or work too hard. It doesn't mean it is a disease. We decide to control our tendencies. I know I have a tendency to think too much about situations. I look at too many angles all the time. Maybe that's why I understand all too well where you're coming from today."

"So you obsess, huh, Doc? So what about my decision to come here? Why did I do that?"

"Accept the obvious and simple first. At the time, it was a decision you thought would improve your life. Simple and obvious. Does that work? If so, don't look any further."

"It makes sense. Why did I decide to have an affair?"

"You answer that. Remember the obvious. If it was a snake, you'd have fang marks on your nose."

"Okay, I guess I thought an affair would be fun and make me feel better. Simple, obvious, no fang marks."

"Simple, obvious, and don't look for insights that don't lead to some action."

"So, if I say I'm from a dysfunctional family and that helps me shape the way I treat my family, then it's good. Or if it tells me about my tendencies and helps me set goals to behave in a certain way, then it's good too. But, if being from a dysfunctional family only leads me to believe that I now know why I'm messed up, then I'm complicating life, not accepting parsimonious explanations for present behavior, and I'm unsettling myself. Hey, Doc, I'm getting good at this. Maybe I'll be a therapist one day."

"You are getting good, Mike. And you are a therapist already. Your own."

"Well, since I'm a therapist, tell me about your obsessiveness. Are you thinking too much about things right now?"

"No Mike, not now. You might say, right now I'm in remission."

EXERCISES

One downside of self-help work in psychology is the tendency to overutilize labels to explain patterns of behavior. An English statesman named John Morley once said, "Labels are devices for saving talkative persons the trouble of thinking." I agree, adding that labels tend to enslave people to the toils of self-analysis. Labels do, however, sell books and self-help programs and have become part of the process in the second session of convincing people they "need" something when they really do not.

Overanalysis is very complicating and is usually a fast ride to misery. As journalist Karl Kraus remarked, sometimes "… psychoanalysis is the illness it purports to cure."

The exercises that follow will help you understand the concepts of labeling and overanalysis. Mike's responses to the exercises are included at the end of this chapter.

Exercise 1

Describe a time when you overanalyzed something, only to find that the solution was much more obvious than the way you analyzed it. This exercise is very similar to when you recognized misinterpreted intentions in the previous session. Try to make this example relate directly to yourself, such as when you assumed there was a failure or a problem between yourself and someone else that just wasn't there. Recognize the feelings you had when you were in the process of analyzing the situation.

Exercise 2

List all the labels and terms you can think of that people use to describe someone else's problems. Terms like "commitmentphobic," "rage-aholic," "codependent," "inner child," and so forth. If you are using an old dictionary, you may be surprised at how few of these words are in it. Many are the creations of pop psychology movements that have the goal of making money. Labels complicate life. They also tend to make us act in ways to fit the pattern described. For instance, if we have two or three of the five symptoms listed for a label, we may develop the rest of the symptoms just because we feel we are *supposed* to. In addition, labels also tend to give a permanence to our problems.

Exercise 3

Take a problem you are experiencing right now, for example, low self-esteem, a weight problem, or an overcomplicated life. Think of at least three possible explanations for your behavior based on the idea that you may be overanalyzing your life. Make your analysis as bizarre as you want. After you have finished, look to the simplest explanations. For example, in this book we are discussing the tendency to overcomplicate life. Explanations could be based on the parents' relationship, toilet training, sexual impulses, or whatever.

Exercise 4

List three tendencies that you have, similar to the way I mention my tendency to obsess. Remember, list them simply as tendencies—do not analyze your reasons for these tendencies.

1. _____

2. _____

3. _____

MIKE'S RESPONSES TO EXERCISES

Exercise 1

I remember when I was first dating my wife, all of a sudden she seemed to disappear. I called for five or six days and she didn't return my calls. I figured it was just one of those things where I pissed her off or something and she didn't want to see me no more. So I gave up. A couple of days later I remember that she had gone on this outdoor trip with a couple of her friends and I had just forgotten. She didn't have a phone to call. I felt like a real jerk, first, because I had forgotten her trip, and secondly, because I was freaking out.

Exercise 2

Labels: rage-aholic, codependent, hyperactive, dysfunctional, inner child, commitmentphobic, Peter Pan syndrome, love addicted, fear of success, fear of failure, type A personality, risk addict, over-enmeshed

Exercise 3

My problem is that I have over-complicated my life. I could say it was because of an early childhood trauma caused by not getting the toys I wanted for Christmas, therefore I decided I would have everything I wanted when I got older. I could say I became complicated because my parents lived a simple life and I had to rebel against them. Or I could say I got over-complicated because I had a dream that I saw a UFO when I was younger and it probably wasn't a dream, but a real UFO that put some type of alien curse on me to make me buy things and think wrong. I guess I should accept that I've complicated my life, realize that perhaps there might be a number of causes, not the least of which is natural human tendencies, then decide just to change it.

Exercise 4

I have a tendency to obsess also. I have a tendency to want my pleasures immediately rather than try to delay them. I have a tendency to make quick decisions when I am emotional that often are destructive. I also tend to run away from relationship problems, rather than be patient enough to solve them.

SESSION 10

Nothing Better than a Bad Time

I got a phone call from the union representative in Mike's precinct only a couple of days after Mike's last session. Mike had shot someone. No one was sure how to react. No one was sure how Mike had reacted. He was being questioned by internal affairs. They wanted to bring him to my office as soon as he was finished. Little did they know, Mike was lucky because he had already been to my office, already had a therapeutic relationship. A cop who doesn't know the police shrink in advance sometimes has trouble talking. He doesn't get the benefit. Mike was lucky. Mike was unlucky.

In all of the electronic media cop stories, I've never seen one adequately show what happens to the cop who shoots someone. In many movies, the killing of the bad guy is a victory—the cop feels elated, victorious. But it doesn't happen that way in real life.

Police psychologists call when an officer kills or is involved in any type of traumatic event, a "critical incident". Critical incidents require a response, because often an officer can have a wave of intense emotion that he doesn't understand. And if critical incidents are not responded to correctly, many times they can trigger any number of breakdowns in the officer's life. Without a proper response, shooting can precipitate intense stress reactions, perceptual distortions, and even breakup of families. Sometimes the reaction to the incident can be delayed by many months, sometimes it is immediate.

We all have critical incidents in our lives—divorces, deaths, other types of trauma. Responding to our critical incidents is as important as responding to Mike's. If we are not responded to, trouble can follow.

Mike came in about two days after the shooting. Usually you try to talk to the person right away. He wanted to go home first to process what had happened. He was very silent, very solemn, and took a long time to get used to being in the room again. The session that follows is a condensed version of a meeting that spread over many hours.

"Mike, I got a call from Tommy telling me a little of what happened the other day. He doesn't know that I already know you, if you don't want to tell him. We've got some very important work to do today to process and debrief the event. Some of it might be really painful, but it is very important. We're just going to talk about the event, talk about your reaction, and clear up any confusion in what you might have remembered, thought, and felt. Then I'll try to give you some information to get you through this. We have as much time as we need today, and we can continue tomorrow if we have to. Just try your best to ..."

"I'll be all right with this, Doc. You don't have to worry about me."

"I know you'll be all right, Mike. You're a tough bugger, but maybe we can talk and help you be all right a little sooner. Start by telling me what you remember—the facts, the way you saw it. The facts ma'am, just the facts."

"I used to love that show. Anyway, God, I've told this story enough the last few days. My partner and I get a call. Gunshot sounds from down by the beach. We figure it's probably a couple of kids setting off firecrackers. So we go down there, sort of routine. We park the car and have to walk over and around this little dune to see the beach. We hear a couple of drunk guys screaming and joking, so we don't think much of it. Well, we walk around this patch of saw grass and see these two drunk guys shooting birds with a couple of shotguns out over the water, yelling and having a good time. My partner yells to them that he's a police officer and to drop the guns. The guy closest to me drops his gun immediately and starts talking, 'No problem, officer. Just fooling around.' The other guy just keeps pointing the gun over the water. This is where it gets weird, like in slow motion. We both yell at him to drop the gun, and he doesn't move. I draw my gun and start screaming, 'Please drop the gun! Don't make anything happen you don't want.' My partner starts moving toward him. His friend is yelling for him to drop the gun, and he shoots it one time right into the air. Then the guy turns toward my partner who's only maybe fifteen feet away and aims the rifle toward him. I think I yelled again but he didn't respond and it was too late, I had to shoot. I caught him about two inches to the left of his left eye, and I guess he died almost instantly."

Mike is very shaken at this point, dazed, on the verge of tears.

"What did you do then?"

"His friend was screaming at me, calling me a killer. He was so drunk you could barely understand him. My partner seemed like he was just staring at me. The kid is just lying in the sand, bleeding."

"What did you do?"

"I went over to the guy. He was just a boy, maybe 22 years old. I checked his neck to see if he had a pulse. He didn't. Then I did one of those weird things that I don't understand. I hit him in the chest and screamed at him. Then I sat down and just stared and I guess my partner called backup 'cause it seemed like a minute later the place was crawling with the whole force. Internal affairs was there asking me all kinds of questions. They took my gun. It was a regular circus."

"What did you scream at him when you hit him?"

"I remember yelling, 'Why did you make me do it? Why did you make me kill you?' I've been sort of in a funk since then. I keep picturing that kid's face. He was only 22 years old."

"Do you remember your thoughts while this was happening?"

"Well, when we first got there I remember thinking it was just a routine call, the kids will drop the guns and we'll drive them home. Then when he wouldn't drop the gun I was thinking, 'What the hell is this kid doing?' It wasn't until the shot in the air that I thought, 'Oh shit, I'm going to have to do something.' When he put the gun sights on my partner I just kept thinking, 'Why is he doing this? I'm going to have to shoot him.' I also thought ...'"

Mike stopped and turned away.

"You also thought ... Something embarrassing."

"Doc, this is messed up. But everything was going in slow motion, and I couldn't help but think how if I shot him my life would get really messed up. I was thinking about my wife and kids and the hell we'd go through. I was thinking how the papers would probably blame me regardless of what happened. I was thinking how this would ruin my chance of ever making detective. I even thought about how you keep saying 'keep life simple' and I knew this would complicate the hell out of my life. I must be really selfish to have these kinds of thoughts right at the time I'm going to kill someone. I mean, it's this kid's life on the line, and I might as well have been singing the Oscar Meyer wiener song. It's disgusting."

I had to chuckle a little. Mike joined in for a little chuckle, too.

"I'll yell at you later for complicating life. Mike, everything you've described is really normal, especially thinking about the consequences of the shooting on you and your family. I guess that thinking about me is a little unusual, but quite a compliment, although I'm not sure if I inspired the wiener song comment. Anyway, distortion of time is also normal because your mind gets so acutely aware in what they call the alarm phase of a reaction to a stressful event. What were your first thoughts afterwards?"

"Like I said, I tried to figure out why he made me do it. Then I sat there thinking I had messed up in some way, and I was trying to think of what I could have done differently."

"What did you come up with? What could you have done differently?"

"I don't have an answer to that yet, but I just feel like I could have done it differently."

"What was the worst part of the event for you?"

"I think it was the look on the kid's face when he had the gun on my partner. He looked demonic, but it seemed like an act, like he was pretending to be bad and was really scared underneath. I keep seeing that face, trying to understand what was going on in his mind. My emotions are so confused. I was angry at first, then upset with myself. Sometimes I'm just confused and guilty. It's weird. I'm not sad, just sort of agitated and nervous, like there's some impending doom about to happen. Look at me, I'm shaking just talking about it."

Mike was shaking. He had a cup of coffee in his hand that he put down because he couldn't hold it still enough to drink.

"Besides seeing the kid's face, what else do you feel in your body?"

"I had this strange reaction at the time it was happening. I could feel my heart beating, and I felt like I couldn't breathe. My muscles were real tight, almost shaky. Afterwards I got this stomachache, and got real cold in my hands. I get the same kind of reaction a couple times a day since, only not as intense. I have dreams about it happening, but they aren't nightmares. Just reliving the damn thing. I also have a little trouble sitting still now, especially when I get the stomach, breathing, and heart-beating feeling. I sort of get real scared when I get the physical stuff, and I think it makes me worse. I'm really a mess, huh, Doc? Am I going crazy?"

"Nah, Mike. So far you are about as normal as you can be. Let me explain some things. When you are faced with a real threatening situation your body goes into an alarm reaction. The alarm reaction is generally the same for most people. In this reaction your heart rate increases, your breathing becomes shallower, your blood vessels pump more blood to your organs and major muscles, and your stomach creates more acid. All these reactions are normal, and actually good for you."

"They don't feel real good. Why are they good? Why do we have them?"

"Well, back when I was a kid and you would walk down the street and a dinosaur came up to you, you knew there was no time to do anything, so you had to either fight it or run from it. Your body had to react, so it would do things to help it react. It would increase the heart rate to pump more blood to the vital organs and major muscles so they'd work better. It would create stomach acid to eat up the food and give you more energy. You would breathe shallower so you get more oxygen in the system. The small capillaries would shut down so you get more blood to the vital parts. All these explain the symptoms you were having, and they actually are the things that helped us survive as a species. So we didn't become dinosaur jerky."

"You realize man wasn't around with the dinosaurs?"

"Well, Mike, I grew up around farms, and a cow looks awfully big to a four-year-old. Anyway, your body acts the same way every time you are under stress, whether the stress is created in your head or you run around the block a few times."

"In other words, I don't need to be afraid of the symptoms?"

"Right. After all, if you had the same symptoms after a good jog, you wouldn't be afraid. You're not going to die from it, and it's not that painful unless you make it painful."

"You know, I actually thought I *would* die from it sometimes. The mind is phenomenal. So the distortion of time is normal, too. What about, well, sometimes I feel like I have tunnel vision? Like I miss what's going on around me 'cause I'm so focused on one thing."

"Also normal. So is distortion of sound."

"Like when I couldn't really make out what the guy's friend was saying. It's nice to know I'm not going crazy."

"Well, I didn't say you weren't crazy before. That's a joke, Mike. You may have remembered some similar reactions when you had other crises."

"Yeah, I can remember feeling this way a few times. Like when I found out my dad died. And when ..."

Mike got a strange look on his face, as if remembering something.

"What just happened, Mike?"

"I was going to say, when I had a relationship break up. I just remembered that the friend at the beach said they got drunk because the guy I shot just had a relationship break up and was really down. I hadn't remembered that before."

"New memories are also normal."

"There's something else I couldn't figure out. He had a double barrel shotgun. Only two shots. When he aimed it at my partner the damn thing was empty. He shot into the air right before he turned, almost like he was emptying it. He had to know the thing was empty. Why would he do something so stupid?"

I was speechless. I had read an article by an FBI guy on this kind of thing. I must have looked strange.

"Doc, are you all right? You just turned white. What happened to you?"

"Sorry, Mike. I've read about these things before but never came close to it."

"What things?"

"Police-assisted suicide. It's possible in his drunken and depressed state, he made a split second decision that he didn't want to live. He may have wanted you to kill him."

Mike was stunned. His breathing became very labored. He stared away, shaking his head for a couple seconds. His voice cracked. He spoke real slow.

"That explains the look I remember on his face. Oh my God. It makes sense. His friend kept saying, 'I should have stopped him.' I thought he meant me. He meant himself."

Mike started to cry.

"How do you feel, Mike?"

"It's weird, I feel sort of relieved, angry, and really bad for those two kids all at the same time. Can I get a couple articles on that?"

"I've got something here in my files."

"It just seems to make sense. It's obvious now. But with tunnel vision I couldn't see it, and no one else really heard the whole story. You know, Doc, something else makes sense. Tunnel vision is normal in this situation, but in the rest of my life I was having tunnel vision, too. That's why I was missing the obvious and simple pleasures."

"Mike, you just did something really, really important."

"What's that?"

"You related this bad situation to the rest of your life and mentioned that it taught you something about yourself. You started trying to figure out what good you were going to get from this situation. You started on the positive side, like a kite rising into the wind."

"I did that? I came in here just worried about how I messed up."

"Mike, I need to hear you say something."

"I don't understand."

"I need to hear you say to me, 'I did the best I could.' Just say that for me and mean it."

"That's tough, but I can say I did the best I could at the time, given the situation."

"Say it again, three times!"

"I did the best I could given the situation. I did the best I could given the situation. You know Doc, I *did* do the best I could. What else can we expect from ourselves? We don't get in these kinds of situations often, maybe once in a life. How are we expected to react to a situation we've never experienced before? We do whatever we can. I did the best I could. I wanted it to turn out better, but dammit, I did the best I could."

"And now we go on."

"And now we go on. Oh shit, I'm really up against it. The press wants to blame me. The department is investigating me. This is going to really be a battle. This could ruin my career and my life."

"Mike, listen to me closely: It's not the bad things that happen to us that determine our lives, it's the way we react to them. Reaction determines outcome, not events."

"I think I missed that."

"Reaction determines outcome, not events. If a bad thing happens to you, and you react in a positive fashion you can usually get some good out of it. In business, the way for a company to come out of nowhere and succeed is to react positively to a bad situation in the industry. It happens over and over."

"So what I do now is more important. How does that apply here?"

"Well, you are about to get a lot of attention. Put the attention to work for you. Show other people who will be looking at you closely what kind of man you are. Go out of your way to cooperate. Help them find the solution. Tell them about police-assisted suicide. Give them an article or two. Show them that you are a good investigator, a hard worker, and a caring man."

"That makes sense. But I feel like I have to defend myself."

"You did the best you could, there's nothing to defend. Be straight-forward. As far as the rest of your life, use the energy created by this incident to rekindle some caring and support at home. Use the time off to get closer to your family. Make the situation you are overcoming a team effort on the part of your family. Make it work for you. I often find that a bad event can bring the positive out in people."

"Including me, if I let it."

"That's right. There's nothing better than a bad time. I know in my own life the worst thing that ever happened to me turned out to be one of the best things that ever happened to me."

"You know, I can get a lot of attention. I will be seen by the people who make the decisions for promotion. I can help my family by being strong now. I just have to focus on what I am doing next, not what happened already."

"If you focus forward, adversity can work for you. There are four simple steps to dealing with a bad situation, Mike. Figure out what this by-product situation will cause, such as attention. Figure out how to turn that by-product—attention—positive. Figure out who can work with you and what relationships can be strengthened. Finally, keep yourself focused on the future, not what happened. Make a goal and a plan to get there based on the situation. 'Sweet are the uses of adversity, Which like a toad, ugly and venomous, Wears yet a precious jewel in his head.' Shakespeare, Mike, from *As You Like It*."

" 'By trying we easily can endure adversity.' Another man's—Mark Twain, Doc."

" 'That which does not kill me makes me stronger.' Nietzsche, Mike."

"Okay Doc, how about, 'When an elephant is in trouble, even a frog will kick him.' Hindu proverb, try that one."

"When did you start getting into quotes, Mike?"

"I knew you'd hit me with at least one when I told you this story, so I went and looked a couple up so I could use them against you, Doc."

"Okay, how about this one. 'Make something good happen out of this or I'll kick your ass.' "

"Who's that, Bronson? John Wayne?"

"That one's mine, Mike. It's all mine."

EXERCISE

Rarely have I heard a success story that didn't include at least one or more adverse events in the person's life. Many times it is the person's reaction to the adversity that gives him the impetus to be more successful and reach to higher heights. While adversity usually opens up new opportunities, it is often when our mental state is at its worst, and we are unable to utilize those opportunities. Healthy people do not smile through adversity, but they do have an ability to keep focused through it. By keeping focused, they leave themselves open to the good things that can happen.

If we respond to adversity by throwing away our stability, our lives will become very complicated. If we are to keep our lives simple, a plan for handling adversity is essential. A few actions are necessary for success in handling adverse situations:

First, see beyond the situation to a time when it will be over. Allow the problem to be "time limited." Too many people believe that when a bad thing happens, life is over, changed for the worse, forever. Adversity is "time limited," at least in the magnitude of its impact on our lives, unless we continue to keep the adverse situation alive.

Second, if you figure out a way to make the adverse situation work for you, you will keep focused on establishing a new life, a benefit. Always remember the previous principle of cutting your emotional losses. Ask yourself: If I am going to lose in this adverse situation, how can I still make the situation work to my advantage? How can I end up as far ahead as possible? If you keep this mind-set, you will handle adversity much more simply and not let it over-complicate your life.

The four steps toward gaining advantage from adversity are:

1. Figure out what the by-products of the situation will be in your life.
2. Figure out how to make that by-product positive.
3. Figure out who will be there with you and what relationships can be strengthened.
4. Make a plan and a goal for benefiting from the situation and keep focused on that goal.

Here are the instructions for completing an adversity worksheet which will ingrain these principles into a system for you. A completed worksheet of Mike's responses is also provided at the end of the chapter.

1. Describe an adverse situation that has happened to you. Try to pick a situation that you did not necessarily create, but was thrust upon you. At this point it is best to not pick something you are going through right now.

2. In the second section, ask yourself what the by-products of that situation were. Every situation has by-products that are not necessarily bad, but that in fact may turn out to be good. Do not list good or bad things that actually happened, just by-products that were caused by the adversity. For example, being fired from your job may have caused you to spend more time at home, have more free time, get more phone calls from your friends, elicit support from your spouse, and so forth. List these responses in this section.

3. Determine who could have been there with you and what relationships could have been strengthened. A strengthened, healthy relationship is always an asset. Look at the people in your life whom you could have reached out to in this situation. Sometimes adversity is a good test of who has a healthy attitude toward friendship.

4. What kind of goal or plan could you have chosen in this situation to make it positive? It does not have to be what happened, but try to decide what you would have done if it were to happen now, rather than before you learned about adversity. Remember, when

looking back do not be hard on yourself over mistakes. Stay future-oriented and use the exercise to learn for the next time.

5. Go through steps 1 through 4 for Mike's situation in this chapter.

ADVERSITY WORKSHEET

Describe an adverse situation that has happened in your life.

What were the by-products of that situation?

What relationships could have been strengthened during this adversity?

What kind of goal or plan could you have made in this situation to make it more positive?

MIKE'S ADVERSITY WORKSHEET

Describe an adverse situation that has happened in your life.
It was about fifteen years ago and my first wife and I were having real problems. We had tried to stay together, even went to counseling, and she finally decided she wanted out. This started the whole divorce process, which became very bitter.

What were the by-products of that situation?
I had to look for a new place and eventually bought a place with a rental apartment, that I re-sold later for a profit.

I was left with a lot of free time which, if I had been focused, I could have put to some good use, especially because I had all this energy going with all that was happening. I also met with a couple of lawyers and accountants who continue to be good resources for me today.

I learned about how the justice system treats these kind of cases and have talked with a number of guys on the job when they were in a similar situation, maybe even saved some of them a lot of hassles.

What relationships could have been strengthened during this adversity?
As we were going through the divorce a lot of people tried to reach out to me. I got invited to a lot of my married friends' houses for dinner, even my own sister reached out to me for the first time in years. We hadn't been talking. Unfortunately, I didn't accept a lot of invitations

because I was a little down. I did, however, get back together with my sister and we've been close ever since.

What kind of goal or plan could you have made in this situation to make it more positive?

I would have liked to use the opportunity to establish a lot closer friendships. I also think it would have been a good time to start something like a real estate business, or a program for officers going through divorce. I could have even written a handbook on getting through a divorce.

SESSION 11

If the Lens Ain't Focused, Don't Snap the Picture

People always say that if they could live life over they would avoid the problems they had the first time through. It's scary to think that in my own life if I avoided the problems and avoided the pain, I would never have accomplished much of anything. The real challenge is to remain focused in the face of problems, to use problems as a guide to finding direction and simplifying. This session is about how Mike remained focused.

Mike called me almost every day with some good news this week. He was as excited as a little boy. He dealt openly with his shooting with everyone around. At first, internal affairs tried hard to put him on the defensive, but he remained very genuine, he educated his superiors about the shooting with articles he had found and gotten from me, he even posed the theory about a police-assisted suicide. The police information officer released the suicide idea to the papers. A very pro-cop article came out of it and made the department look real good. Suddenly, as they started to look good, they left Mike alone. Funny how that works.

At times, Mike brought up his feelings about having killed someone, and he dealt with himself in as genuine a fashion as he had dealt with others. He was almost a half-hour early for his session, and he kept checking to see if the patient before him had left. Finally, his turn came, about ten minutes before his appointment time.

"Doc, I couldn't wait to see you today. Do you believe what has been happening? I've gotten such support from everybody. I even got a note from the commissioner saying stuff about the difficult times being a police officer. I didn't care what it said; it was just good to know he wasn't too busy to think about me. The inspector called me in and gave me this whole talk about how good my record was. He was so interested in the articles I gave him. He was also interested in how willing I was to go to the debriefing with you. He actually sounded a little like you when he told me that sometimes good things come from bad events. I just can't believe what happened."

"Mike, it didn't happen to you. You reacted well to the event, and your reaction is being well received. Reactions determine outcomes to adverse situations."

"Okay, maybe I deserve some credit, but all I'm doing is talking with people and sharing the experience. They're even talking about having me talk to others when something like this happens to them."

"In business, they call talking to other people networking. It's how people get ahead. People don't just jump ahead, they get lifted by others. How are you handling the event in your own mind?"

"Well, that's a bit of a problem still. As I get attention, I feel a little guilty at times. I mean, here I am reaping the benefits, while I killed someone who wasn't doing anything but acting out a depression. I mean, he was just a kid, not much older than my kid. It's not fair to his family. He died for no reason."

"Not fair?"

"Intellectually I know that fairness is relative, but what do I do about that when the feeling comes?"

There's no answer to this question. As a psychologist we always want to have an answer, though. Sometimes just a sympathetic face is all I have in me.

"No response, Doc."

"Mike, there's no answer. You did the best you could at the time. You didn't create the situation. You didn't even have much time to think about it. Now you either focus yourself and move on, or not. It's your choice. Fight the feeling with the phrases you already know. It's that simple."

"Simple. There's your word again. Doc ... Doc ..."

A long stare into space, open-mouthed pause.

"Mike?"

"Doc, sometimes I just don't want it to be simple. I know simple is better. You've convinced me of that. But, I just don't want it to be that way. No, actually, I think simple is so unnatural for me that it actually gets complicated because I have to think about it a lot. Yeah, that's it. I have to think too hard to be simple."

Mike starts laughing real hard at himself. It was contagious, so I started laughing a little, too.

"Doc, you're going to love this one. Over the last couple of weeks I went to play golf a few times. They gave me the time off so I played some more golf. And I thought to myself, what would make this game simple. So I started focusing on just one thing. I pretended that my club, whatever club I was using, was part of my backbone. I kept my club in line with my backbone and just swung. I stopped worrying about my grip and my stance and thinking inside-out on the swing and the thousands of other things I keep saying to myself. I just thought, keep the club in line with the backbone. And, dammit, I scored a 92 the first round and a 87 the second round, and the next two rounds have been in the 80's also. I hadn't scored below a 98 the last couple of years."

(This is, of course, an aberration. I've played golf for years and don't score in the 80's. If anyone could simplify the game, it would be me. You can't lower a score almost ten points by just a thought process. It's not even worth my time discussing. But, if he thinks it works, all the power to him. I'll relate to him on his level.)

"Well, Mike, see what can happen if you focus on simplicity? Remember, simplifying means giving up. You gave up all the neurotic corrections you kept making that complicated and ruined your game. You are doing the same with your life."

(I had this irresistible urge to go to the driving range. Nah, it couldn't work.)

"Doc, I think focus is the problem. We've spent three months simplifying, and I think I'm just having trouble putting it all together. It's sometimes a little fuzzy."

"If the lens ain't focused, don't snap the picture."

"How do I focus?"

"Focusing is easy, Mike. Let's start by reviewing what you remember from the sessions."

"Well, we started off talking about how people complicate their lives by believing that more is better, that people try to build and build without a strong foundation. All they end up doing is complicating their lives ..."

(On my course there's this long par 5 with an approach shot over the water. I bet the backbone thing would work there.)

"... Then you showed me that we have to rebuild a simple life from the bottom up by first simplifying things, then thoughts, relationships, and spirituality. We've worked on things and thoughts, and, believe me, I'm ready for the relationship discussions. Simplicity is a matter of letting go. That seems to be the basic concept. Are you following me, Doc?"

(I think Mike noticed that I was subtly flicking my pen as if it were a golf club. I'd better calm down.)

"Yeah, Mike. I'm listening. Letting go, right. You got it. Go on."

"With things, we talked about how to reduce the feeling that you 'need' things to be happy or have status. Basic needs are very simple. Then we discussed escaping complicating clutter, valuing time not money, reducing the flow of money and the use of credit, and, finally, finding that goals in life can be the secret to control desires."

(I wonder if it works for putting, too. My putting has been really bad. Let's see. Backbone straight, club in line, visualize ...)

"Next, we worked on thoughts. Reducing extremes, mental pinballing, looking to the simple and obvious explanations first. Finally, we dealt with how an adverse situation can be used to your benefit. That's where I am right now. You know, Doc, I guess it really isn't that hard to simplify."

"It's hard to make it permanently a part of you. I want you to do something with me now. I want you to make a personal commitment statement, a written document of what you are committed to do for yourself now."

Jokingly. "You want to commit me?"

"Sort of. I want to put down some personal promises stating how you will not complicate your life again. We'll add to it after we work on relationships and spirituality. Right now, let's get you focused."

"How do I start?"

"The first statement on your personal commitment statement should be an overall acclamation about how you want to live your life."

"Well, I want to live my life as simply as possible, while exploring new parts of my world. I want to dedicate myself to valuing the simple pleasures in life, the relationships with my family and friends. I want ..."

"Just a second, Mike. I have to write this stuff down for you. I'm just going to change one word, because this is a commitment statement. I 'will,' 'not want to,' live my life as simply as possible while exploring new parts of my world."

"I like that. I will."

(I will simplify my own golf game. I will try the backbone thing. Dammit, why did he have to apply my concepts to a golf game? Why didn't I ever think about that?!)

"What else, Mike? Use the concepts you have learned."

"I will reduce my need for things so that I am not desperate when I make decisions. I will stop looking to things as a way of gaining happiness or status. I will keep my finances in check by rarely using credit and keeping my use of checks to a bare minimum. I will stop cluttering my house with things, and twice a year reduce the clutter that is there. No wait, change that from 'stop cluttering my house' to 'stop cluttering my life.'"

"Now you're on a roll, Mike."

"I will value time above all. I will make purchasing decisions on the basis of time spent. I will strive to do what is on my wish list and keep my wish list up to date. I will stop using extreme words in my thought and language. I will stop defending myself to please others. I will look to the most simple and obvious solution first and accept it if I can. I will stick to the task at hand when faced with adversity."

"Is that it?"

"Can I add one that we never discussed, Doc? I think it complicates life tremendously."

"Go ahead."

"I will not lie or engage in an activity that I have to lie about—no more affairs for me."

"Lying is maybe one of the most complicating factors in life. You are getting very good at this simplicity stuff, Mike."

"Yeah, I am. And I feel very proud that I'm getting good."

"You should be proud, Mike. I bet it feels good for you to 'show off' to me."

"Actually, it does."

"In that case, I'm going to put myself out a little, and let you show off some more. I don't have another appointment the next hour, and there's a driving range just down the road. As a therapeutic tool, I'm going to go with you and let you 'show off' how your golf game has gotten better."

"But Doc, I don't have my ..."

"I have my clubs in the car. It will be good for you, Mike. You can 'show off' the backbone thing. It's therapeutic."

Mike smiles knowingly.

"Therapeutic, huh, Doc? Well, I am free, but I don't know if I want to show anyone my technique. Who knows, I might do one of those golf videos or something."

"Let's go out and get in the car, Mike, before I wrap a graphite shaft driver around your neck."

"Now there's a *simple* choice, Doc."

EXERCISE

One tradition that bothers me is the New Year's resolution—the yearly tradition where people commit to change and usually break the commitment(s) within a couple of weeks. Initially, people are completely focused on their resolutions, but once they are no longer the focus of their lives, they go by the wayside. The status quo returns. Sometimes therapy is no more than extended New Year's resolutions. The change happens in sessions, but slowly the old habits resurface. The personal commitment statement is one way to overcome the tendency to let things return to the status quo.

A good personal commitment statement lists day-to-day behavior and general guides for thoughts, possessions, relationships, and spirituality. We will start one here, but you should add to it as you go along. Now for the important part: At the beginning, read your personal commitment statement at least once a day, twice if possible. After a few months—not days but months—you can slowly reduce that to once a week. If you do not read the statement frequently, it will not become ingrained in your mind, and will most likely go the direction of New Year's resolutions. Reading it once a day will start you on the road to a simpler life.

Mike's personal commitment statement read like this:

- I will live my life as simply as possible while exploring new parts of my world.
- I will dedicate myself to valuing the simple pleasures in life and relationships with my family and friends.
- I will reduce my need for "things" so that I am not desperate when I make decisions.
- I will stop looking to things as a way of gaining happiness or status.
- I will keep my finances in check by rarely using credit and keeping my use of checks to a bare minimum.
- I will stop cluttering my life with things, and twice a year reduce the clutter in it.
- I will value time above all.
- I will make purchase decisions on the basis of time spent.
- I will strive to do what is on my wish list and keep my wish list up to date.
- I will stop using extreme words in my thoughts and language.
- I will stop defending myself to please others.
- I will look to the most simple and obvious solution first, and accept it if I can.
- I will stick to the task at hand when faced with adversity.
- I will not lie or engage in any activities that I have to lie about—no more affairs.

1. Now it's your turn. Fill out the Personal Commitment Statement that follows. The first step is to make an overall statement about how you want to live your life. You can make more than one statement if you want, just do not put too much in each statement. You want this Personal Commitment Statement to be simple.

2. Next, fill out the section that says "things." Make a number of statements about how you will determine the role of possessions in your life. You may want to look at the review section from the last session, but you are certainly not limited to what is written in this book. Remember, this book is a guide to help you find your way, so feel free to add your own touches to this list.

3. Fill out the section under thoughts. Again, you may wish to review the summary section, or individual chapters. Try to include a plan for dealing with adversity, noting what you will do if you stray from the life you want to lead.

4. Add any other statements you wish to make. I want you to return to this list after you read the next two sections and add more statements regarding relationships and spirituality.

5. Most importantly, look at this list at least once every day for the next three months. Read it, and make your commitment to yourself.

MY PERSONAL COMMITMENT TO MYSELF

Overall statement(s) of how I want to live my life

Things
What is the role of things in my life?
How will I control my finances?
What kind of activities do I want to spend my time on?
What will I work on from my wish list?
Your commitment statements about things:

_____

_____

_____

_____

_____

Thoughts
What will I say to myself and not say to myself anymore?
What role will expectations play in my life?
What is the role of analysis?

How will I handle adversity?
Your commitment statements about thoughts:

_____

_____

_____

_____

_____

Other personal commitment statements:

_____

_____

_____

_____

_____

SUMMARY OF SIMPLIFYING THOUGHTS

Five steps:

1. Learn to cut your emotional losses. Do not allow extremeness in your vocabulary and self-talk.

2. Avoid mental pinballing. Recognize that you can't meet everyone's expectations because people and their expectations are not consistent. If more is expected of you than is possible, let the other people decide based upon your choices. Never defend yourself against their expectations.

3. Do not overanalyze. Accept the simplest explanation possible for events.

4. Have a plan for handling adversity. Stay future-oriented, and look for the potential advantages that can be gained from a bad situation.

5. Have a personal commitment to yourself, written and kept where you can review it regularly.

SESSION 12

You're OK, I'm a Jerk

*I*nvolvement in relationships can easily be one of the most difficult aspects of our lives. The purity and resolve of the human spirit is most tested when dealing with people closest to us. Love and friendship are basic human strivings. We started as pack animals and continue to be so. And it is those animals in our pack that we are most likely to give the power over our happiness and despair, our progress or futility, and sometimes even our life and death.

You can't begin to simplify your relationships until you are simplified yourself. The area of relationships tests Mike most, as it does most people. Shift work, forced overtime, and isolation from society all render his relationships more complicated, not to mention the possibility that he could lose his life any day on the job. It is also difficult for him to share his feelings about his job with those who are not cops, so friendships are more difficult under these conditions. And a police officer's spouse tends to take on more responsibilities at home, and may also have a difficult time relating to his day-to-day work life. This separatism can facilitate a gap between two people. When this gap gets misinterpreted, as most gaps do, complications occur, and the relationship suffers.

Mike came to the session a little early. He was in the waiting room trying to busy himself with a magazine or two.

"Come on in, Mike."

"You need some better waiting room magazines."

"Let's see. I have *Sports Illustrated*, police magazines, gun magazines, travel magazines, *People*, *New York* magazine, cooking magazines, financial magazines, science magazines, some geographical stuff, and kiddie magazines. I guess I am missing *Toe Grooming Weekly*, but the selection isn't that bad."

"You know, I noticed just now that you never defend yourself. You just have a way of putting someone in his place when he tries to criticize. It's a humor thing; keeping a sense of humor when someone is critical of you disarms people. It's like, you don't have to get defensive if you have other weapons. I think ..."

"Mike, calm down. Let's go into my office. What's up today? It's unlike you to go on like that."

"I guess I didn't see anything I wanted to read."

"Right, Mike. What's going on?"

"I don't know. I'm feeling a little nervous today. Sort of like I used to when I first started coming."

"Relationships—must be a tough topic for you."

"That's the simplest explanation, I guess. OK, how do we do this?"

"Slowly, Mike, slowly. Relax and slow down. First, Mike, I want you to do an exercise with me. I'm going to give you some situations. I want you to rate how the situation makes you feel about yourself. Rate it on a +10 to -10 scale, with +10 being you feel really good about yourself and -10 being you feel really bad about yourself."

"Let me get this right: +10 makes me feel really good about myself; +5 makes me feel a little better about myself; -5 or -4 or -3 means I'm feeling a little bad about myself; and a -9 or -10 would be if I have a really bad feeling about myself."

"You got it, Mike. Plus ten to minus ten. Zero means it doesn't change the way you feel about yourself. Okay, first situation: You get a really low grade on a test for a class you were taking."

"OK. Let's see, that would depend a little on how important the test was, but I guess I'd feel pretty bad, so I'll give that a -7."

"OK a -7. How about if you get a good grade on a test?"

"Maybe a +4 or so."

"How about if you got the highest grade in the class on a test?"

"That would boost it to maybe a +7."

"Now, how about if your boss blames you for a problem at work where you messed up?"

"Maybe a -9, even a -10. I mean, particularly if I did mess up."

"How about if the boss calls you in and tells you that you're a good cop, like he did last week?"

"That is a +8. I've got the idea. I'm more critical of a bad situation than I am positive toward a good situation."

"You *don't* have it, Mike. Just try to do the exercise. I'll explain later. How about if you come home and your wife says she loves you?"

"That's a +9 or +10."

"Say you come home and you and your wife get into a fight and she calls you some nasty names?"

"I'd give that a -9 or -10."

"How about if the newspaper gets delivered on Sunday like it's supposed to?"

"What, that's stupid. That doesn't change how I feel about myself. That's a zero."

"Now, how do you rate when a driver cuts you off in his car? How does that change the way you feel about yourself?"

"Now you're getting tricky. I *do* get a little angry, but I don't really change the way I feel about myself. So that's a zero."

Mike pauses a second and gets a confused look on his face.

"What's the strange look for Mike?"

"I don't know. I know I'm getting something here, but I'm not sure what."

"How does it change the way you *feel about yourself* when your kid does something good in school?"

"I feel good as a parent, maybe even feel a little better about myself. A +3 or +4 perhaps."

"Let me shift the question. Rate for me how much change you feel about your *kid* when he does better in school?"

"Well, I always love my kids. I'd feel good for him, but I wouldn't love him more. So that has to be a zero."

"How do you feel about a friend if he gets yelled at by his boss?"

"Sonofabitch. It doesn't change the way I feel about a friend, or my wife, or even a stranger, if they fail. It bothers me about myself. I change the way I feel about myself when something bad happens, but not usually about other people. If someone else fails a test, I might even feel more positive toward them, or pity them. What's going on? What is this supposed to mean?"

"Mike, it means that we tend to be very judgmental about ourselves when we fail, even more than we would of other people. I call it the 'You're Okay, I'm a Jerk' philosophy. It's a natural tendency in a lot of people."

Mike has this very pensive look, like a kid discovering there really is no Santa Claus.

"Mike, when our self-esteem is dependent on our failures and successes we will go up and down just like you did on this test. Making our self-esteem dependent on accomplishment creates a very complicated sense of self. Self-esteem that is independent is simple."

"It goes back to what you were saying before, after the shooting—I must be able to say I did the best I can."

"You got it. Effort is the better measure of self. Back to that old adage your parents told you."

"It's not whether you win or lose, it's how you play the game."

"Wasn't so simple then, Mike. You can control effort, but not outcome."

"And if my effort is not as good as I'd like it to be, then perhaps there are other intervening circumstances that I have to work on first, parts of my personality or tendencies that I have to control first. I've got the idea, Doc. Control the tendencies, then give full effort. Gauge your esteem around effort, not success. Increase effort by controlling the tendencies that reduce effort."

"So what happens if you fail a test, Mike?"

"First, I say I did the best I could given the situation. Then, I figure out how I can rearrange my life if I choose to better the situation for more effort next time. But what if I still feel down?"

"Mike, the first two steps are good and simple. One, say I did the best I could. Two, figure out if you can improve the situation in the future to give more effort. The last step is to make it a zero."

"A zero."

"Remember the exercise. Make it a zero. Say it to yourself, say it out loud if you have to, scream the damn thing, say that this doesn't change the way you feel about yourself. It's a zero. I'm not better or worse because of this, I'm still me."

"Make it a zero. OK, that makes sense. But what does this have to do with relationships? Seems like we are still on me."

"Mike, suppose you are in a relationship, and you vacillate very strongly about how you feel about yourself, who would be the first person to hear it?"

"Whoever I am closest to, I guess."

"In that case, there would be a strain on the relationship. If the relationship centers too much around one person's vacillations, it will be somewhat tenuous. If all the energy in a relationship is spent trying to steady the relationship, it will get very complicated. Now, if you feel poorly about yourself, are you likely to take risks?"

"No! Taking risks requires confidence."

"If there are no risks then there will be a tendency to stagnate in the same pattern. What would that do for a relationship?"

"I guess that's what people mean by living in a rut."

"Precisely. Variety requires not only energy, but also confidence to take risks. Now, if you are in a relationship and feel less of a person every time the other person gets angry at you, what is going to happen?"

"I'll just feel worse and worse about myself and look to find ways to feel better about myself. That's when I'd look to other people. So, at least one person in every relationship must have a steady sense of self-esteem that is not dependent on situations."

"Very good. The criticism cycle starts when, every time one person criticizes the other, he feels down on himself. Then you just want to escape."

"That explains why sometimes I would rather be at work than be at home. Work allowed me to feel better about myself. That explains my affairs. All this time I was blaming my wives, when really I was letting them affect my sense of self."

"The chances are you won't be in a successful relationship until you stop judging yourself. Working on self-judgments is the first step to making your relationships simpler."

Mike had a big grin on his face.

"You know, Doc, I feel better about myself already having understood this concept. In fact, I'm probably a +8 or +9 right now."

He was proud of his little joke.

"I gotta get out of this shrink business. Maybe I could sell those little pet turtles in Florida ... "

EXERCISES

In the course of simplifying your relationships you will encounter many setbacks. Whenever you involve someone else in the process, it gets more complicated. Remember, people are not consistent in the way they feel. In counseling, it is usually helpful to get the spouse involved in therapy with the patient. In your process of simplifying, perhaps it may be helpful for you to involve the significant people in your life. Just keep working toward the goal of simplicity, and try to be understanding of the shifts of inconsistency.

The first step to having a healthy, simplified relationship is to have a strong sense of self. I don't particularly like the concept of self-esteem because it implies that people have to evaluate themselves to survive. It is not necessary to evaluate yourself, only your efforts and their effects. Life is simplest when your view of yourself is not dependent on the outcome of your efforts. As usual, simplicity seems to hinge on the idea of giving something up. In this case, what you are giving up is the idea of self-evaluation.

The following exercises attempt to help you understand the process of reducing self-evaluation.

Exercise 1

Go through the exercise in the chapter and try to make the following situations a "zero" as far as impacting the way you feel about yourself. Even the positive things should be a zero, because if good things change the way you feel about yourself, bad things will also. This is not to say don't be happy, just don't change your feeling about yourself. You can make them a zero with some of the self-talk discussed at the beginning of the last section or by simply realizing that failure and successes are not the measures that you want to base your self-esteem on.

- You fail a test in a class.
- You get into an argument with your boss over something you didn't do right (in his eyes).
- Your spouse, girlfriend, or boyfriend decides to spend time with his or her friends rather than with you.
- You hear that a proposal you submitted was rejected.
- You didn't get the raise you thought you were supposed to get even though others in your workplace did.
- Your child fails a course in school.
- Your child gets straight A's in school.
- You get a high grade on a test.
- You get an incentive raise at work.

- You win the lottery.
- You can't pay the bills for a month.
- A friend gets angry at you for not calling.
- A friend calls and says he or she misses you.
- You win an award for citizenship.
- A friend buys a car that you always wanted but can't afford.
- Your spouse, girlfriend, or boyfriend calls you a couple of bad names in a fight over something insignificant.
- Your spouse, girlfriend, or boyfriend says "I love you."
- You get a secret admirer letter.
- Someone you don't even know complains about you.
- A friend tells you that a couple of people were talking negatively about you.

Exercise 2

Write down some instances when you were not as successful as you would have wished. Now work on believing that "I did the best I could do." If you don't honestly believe that, figure out what it would have taken for you to do a better job. Sketch this underneath the description of the situation. Then say, "I have gotten the most out of the situation I can at this point." It may seem a rather simplistic exercise, but we can only learn from failures after they occur. We can't change outcomes.

Exercise 3

Spend the next couple of weeks making new situations a "zero," as far as how they affect you. Add these situations to the earlier list. Let your feelings about yourself be derived from within, not from what happens outside.

SESSION 13

I'm OK, You're a Jerk

In addition to my police clientele, I spend a good part of my career working with teenagers. Teenagers have such insecure views of themselves. Many of them try to make themselves feel better by constantly criticizing others. Hours and hours are spent on the phone gossiping, cutting other people down in an attempt to feel better about their own inability to be perfect. The more insecure they feel, the more they criticize. It's a tradition that has driven adults crazy for generations. Even Plato recognized how difficult it was for adults to tolerate teenagers back in his day.

I once had a teenage therapy group where every kid had a different hair color, none of which could be classified as blonde, brunette or redhead. I called them my Day-Glo Coalition—a chameleon's worst nightmare. They also had every body part imaginable pierced or tattooed, including some body parts that I wouldn't let them show me. These kids were constantly criticizing others for judging them on the way they looked, dressed or the music they listened to. "No one loves me anymore," they would complain. What they didn't realize was that they had discouraged everyone who did love them, not by their expressed independence, but by their criticisms and negative attitudes. They pushed the people close to them away. Isn't it great that we grow out of being teenagers? Or do we?

Mike came to this session in uniform, with a hand-held radio in case of an emergency call.

"My turn to get my head shrunk, Doc."

"Shrunk, hell no. I'm just trying to expand your brain a little so it doesn't slip out one of your ears when you're sleeping."

Mike laughs. "Yeah, it would be nice to not have to wear those cotton balls to bed at night anymore. What are we talking about today?"

"The '80–'81 Lakers, the Revolutionary War, and the 'thin blue line.'"

"Great! Real psychology stuff. Ah, the Lakers of the '80s—one of the best squads in history. They won more games in one season than anyone. Magic Johnson, Kareem Abdul Jabbar, Norm Nixon, Jamaal Wilkes. What a dynasty! And you know, Doc, they teach you a lot about relationships."

(I was in total surprise. Could he know where I'm going?)

"How so?"

"I don't have a clue, but I know you're going to relate it somehow. I thought I'd get a head start. What the hell do the L.A. Lakers have to do with me and my wife?"

"Remember, Mike, when we talk about relationships, we're not just talking about you and your wife. We're talking about all your relationships, friendships too. Anyway, the '80–'81 Lakers swept through the play-off to be the NBA champs—the best in the world the year before, Magic Johnson's first year. Everyone picked them to be the first back-to-back champions ever. They had so much talent, how could they lose? They lost that year in the play-offs to a team that had the worst record of any of the play-off teams, under .500. Do you know why?"

"I guess winning went to their heads."

"In a way. Books written about that team claim that newspapers had built up Magic Johnson as some kind of superstar and gave him all the credit for the team success. The others resented it; they started criticizing each other, sometimes even openly in games. When someone would make a mistake they would jump all over them. They became a losing team because of it. When the team turned that around, they started winning again."

Mike was real silent, like he was a bad kid being lectured by the principal.

"Mike, you're real quiet."

"Just thinking. A lot of marriages are that way, Doc. They start off as this winning team, then they start criticizing each other and the team falls apart. In fact, it seems most marriages I know of are that way."

"Maybe that's why our country's divorce rate is so high. Sometimes friendships go that way, too. What happened with the Lakers is that they took a situation and made more out of it than was necessary. They were looking to blame each other for failures, and not looking at themselves. It was an 'I'm OK, you're a jerk' philosophy."

"Doc, I guess they didn't seek the simple explanation—that the media wanted a hero. In marriage, we don't see mistakes as just mistakes, we always put a meaning behind them."

"We always want to believe that other people are more together than we are, and place real deep meaning into every action. Judging other people's actions creates gaps in relationships—it complicates."

"Gotcha. Revolutionary War. I love that time in history. A bunch of rebels pulled together to fight against a seemingly informidable opponent and won. Intelligent tactics, heroes willing to die for a cause, everyone pulling together—what a great start to a nation. It's a shame we don't have that attitude much anymore."

"Even in our own homes, Mike, most people don't have that attitude. What could be simpler? A common goal that you are willing to sacrifice for. A marriage, a friendship—a common bond. Did the Minutemen worry about possessions that much? Did they worry about self-analysis or any other kind of analysis? It doesn't appear that they did. Freedom was more important. Relationships can be our freedom, our bond."

"And I guess the criticisms and arguments can be our Paul Revere, Doc. When the disagreement starts we can hear the British coming and fight for the relationship rather than with each other."

"Very poetic, Mike. I'm going to use that. Very poetic."

"Not bad for a street cop, huh? Now what about the 'thin blue line.' "

"Mike, what is your interpretation of what the 'thin blue line' is?"

"Well, it's the belief that whenever another cop gets into a situation, you believe in him. You protect him because the job frequently requires that you act in ways others might not understand. So you always stand by another cop; you don't air his actions openly. The exception is when he is way out of bounds of the law. But on lesser indiscretions, a fellow cop should be protected."

"Is it a good practice?"

"Well, it's both good and bad. It's good because cops do have demands that aren't understood and can't be afraid to act for fear of their partner turning them in if they make a mistake. So it allows a cop latitude with which to act in a way to protect himself. It also breeds a sense of camaraderie. It's bad because some guys take advantage of it and go way out of bounds, expecting the men and women on the job to protect him. They put people in a bad position, then demand protection under the 'thin blue line.' "

"Do you give your wife the same 'thin blue line'? "

"What do you mean?"

"When a disagreement occurs, or a mistake is made, is it sometimes aired publicly?"

"Well, it doesn't make front page news, but I guess I talk about it with my friends and relatives. I guess I 'air it publicly.' But she does too. Then, I can't let what she does affect what I do."

"Why don't you air a cop's mistakes publicly?"

"I know what you want me to say, dammit, and I guess I have to say it. When something gets aired publicly, life gets complicated. The more people involved, the more complicated it gets. For a cop, they could get raked over the coals by internal affairs, or get jumped on by their superiors. The newspapers can make a mockery of an insignificant situation. It can get real messy. And the same thing happens in your private life. If you air relationship problems publicly, they get more complicated. Seems like it's a teamwork thing, Doc. I guess all these points are about making a better team."

"Keeping your mouth shut about personal stuff makes life simpler, Mike?"

"OK, let me try to put this one together. You can help your relationship thrive if you don't dribble critical words, if you enjoy the common bond, and if you hold that line."

"You are on today, Mike. I've got to give it to you—you are on today."

"Must be the uniform. I know I can always shoot you if you piss me off."

"I'll take my chances. Now I want you to do an exercise with me, Mike. I want you to picture this: You come home from a shift, plus four hours overtime on a last-minute collar. You walk in the door, and your wife starts screaming at you about how you're not spending any time with the family. Got the picture?"

"I don't even have to close my eyes for that one. I live the picture."

"OK, why is she really upset this night rather than other nights?"

"Well, knowing my wife, she's probably upset because one of her meddling friends said something about me not being home."

"OK, give me another explanation or possibility, Mike."

"Well, let's see, the kids were acting up, or she got a call from the school and they blamed her."

"OK, give me five more possible explanations. Let yourself go."

"Damn, let's see. She is unhappy because her mother was nagging at her again. She is angry because she wanted me sexually, and I wasn't there ..."

"I knew you'd throw that one in. Continue."

"She doesn't feel well. Hell, I don't know."

"Two more."

"She's feeling lonely, or saw something on TV that made her feel all alone. Or maybe something went wrong in the house, and I wasn't there to fix it. Or she could have just had a bad day. Or ..."

"You could go on forever, couldn't you? I mean, there could have been a death in the family. Something might have happened to the car. She could just be sitting there analyzing her life and driving herself bonkers. She might have gotten a big phone bill. It's just endless."

"OK, the point, Doc?"

"How do you respond to her yelling at you?"

"I guess that depends why she's upset."

"You're full of it, Mike! You just walk in the door and she's yelling at you. How do you usually respond?"

"I yell back. 'Let me in the damn door first. I don't want to hear it. I just worked a double.' I start a fight."

"Well, we don't need to blame anyone for starting a fight. Now, Mike, what is a response that reflects teamwork? It's not being critical of a teammate, two people having a common cause in life, and holding that protective line. How do you respond to reflect these qualities?"

"I ask if she's all right and I take an interest in what she is telling me. It's common sense, I guess."

"Common sense does not lead to common action."

"Now there's a three-point shot at the buzzer. Common sense definitely does not always lead to common action."

EXERCISES

Teamwork, common goals, and avoiding negative talk about someone is such common sense it's almost cliché when talking about relationships. Given a national divorce rate over 50 percent, it seems that some people are ignoring these simple principles. When someone on your team does poorly, you support them if you want them to continue at full effort. It's that simple. If you are in an argument with someone very close to you, keep it within the relationship, don't take it outside. If you are in a marriage, make sure you have common goals that are well spelled out. Most people *think* they have common goals, but rarely have they actually agreed on them together. The exercises that follow will help you behave in a manner that displays these common sense attitudes.

Exercise 1

Teamwork: List five ways that sports teams or work teams engender closeness and cooperation. Write down how you might apply this behavior to situations in your own home or with a friend.

Exercise 2

Common goals: Share your wish list with someone who is close to you. Talk about what goals you may have in common. If you do this with your spouse or significant other, make a new wish list together.

Exercise 3

Negative talk: Begin by not allowing yourself to listen to negative talk from anyone about your friends. Remember, there is a difference between negative talk and asking for advice about a situation with a friend or spouse. You must make that distinction in your own mind, so do it now before you need it. Describe the last situation you remember where you talked about someone negatively. Now try to re-script the conversation using terms that do not indicate that you are judging this person. Check Mike's work on this exercise to get a good example of how to use non-judgmental language.

Exercise 4

Describe an argument you had with someone over something (that you realize now) was insignificant. Now go back through that argument and determine where you could have expressed teamwork, common goals, and "holding the line" for that person. Look hard—in any argument there's often an opportunity to express all three attitudes, although my experience has shown that expressing just one of them can diffuse the tension quickly.

MIKE'S RESPONSE TO EXERCISES

Exercise 1
Team building

Pep talks from the coach—a regular motivational positive talk with Suzie and the kids might actually go a long way.

Teamwork drills—a basketball team always does a lot of passing and weaving drills to become a team that plays together. Our family could do fire drills and cleaning drills, or "Grandma is coming" drills, and as long as they are playful, they will draw us together.

Team songs and cheers—if we develop certain family favorites that we do over and over it can develop teamwork.

Learning new things together—before we plan to go somewhere we could learn about it together. We can take up a new family sport or activity and learn about it together.

Help each player with their individual weaknesses—good teams pull together to help each individual improve. I can engender this attitude with the family instead of making fun when someone does not do very well.

Exercise 2
Mike and Suzie's wish list together

Improve our relationship
Get kids through college
Set up a comfortable retirement
Go to Venice, Italy
Go to DisneyWorld with the boys
Spend more time together alone
Make more friends and have more dinner parties
Go out dancing at least once a month
Travel across country in a recreation vehicle

Exercise 3

Negative talk

I was talking about the lieutenant to a friend. I was upset about the new department directive to stop overtime use by the officers. I depended on overtime money to pay bills. I was calling the lieutenant a real jerk because he was cutting back in what I thought were the wrong places—like when you do an arrest at the end of your shift and it carries over. I said he was dangerous because he told us not to make any late-shift arrests. I called him an ass-kisser because he did what the big bosses wanted and ignored the men under him.

I could have talked about him feeling pressure and being caught in the middle. After all, he was one of us not long ago. I could have said that he was having trouble meeting the demands of his superiors and being a friendly boss to us. I could have mentioned that pressure will often make people blur the line of the rules. I was angry and I wanted to blame someone.

Exercise 4

Insignificant arguments

I argued terribly with Suzie over her committing us to go to this dinner party with people that neither of us like. I really got on her, bringing up everything from the past. I could have said that we'll do whatever we could to salvage the evening and that we were in it together. I could have suggested we go for a short time, then go out just the two of us to have fun. I could have told her I knew she meant well and must have felt pressured to accept the invitation. If I'd have encouraged these kinds of teamwork thoughts, we probably would have gone, left early, and went out and had a good time together.

SESSION 14

You Aren't Lookin' in the Mirror if the Reflection Isn't You

I remember when I was a little kid and my parents would have an argument, I would get very upset and feel helpless. So I devised this idea: I went to each of them separately and offered them everything in my piggy bank to the first one who would offer to make up. I knew I had to look as cute and as hurt as possible. I was sure it would work, and I was sure they would never take my few pennies of savings. I would just let them know I hurt and gave them a way to get back together while saving face. It worked the first couple of times, so I tried it over and over.

Then, one day, when I was about twelve, I came in from playing and my parents were in separate rooms. Mom told me they had a fight, and that dad was acting stupid again. Dad said mom was being unreasonable and he didn't know what was going to happen, but he was sure there would be no dinner that night. Dinner was the way they knew they could get me. I went to my room and found that my piggy bank was moved from inside my desk to the top of my dresser. A fight no one saw, no dinner, piggy bank on the dresser. I knew a set-up when I saw one.

I cut open the bank, filled it full of marbles, and glued it back together. When I went in to offer it to my dad, he, of course, took it. I went out of the room with a fake cry. Mom and dad quickly discovered the marbles, the double ruse. They came into my room laughing, and asked me why I filled it with marbles. I looked at them and said, "The bank was like your fights, when you really look inside, what's there is not what you expect." Pretty profound for a twelve-year-old, huh? I got the idea from an Aesop's Fable we read in school that week. My parents got this eerie, silent look on their faces, walked out of the room, and made dinner. After that day, I guess I was destined to become a psychologist.

Mike came into my office with a look on his face. He wanted to tell me he was hurt. He wanted me to make something better—I knew I was going to need my piggy bank.

"I can't wait for your explanation of this one, Doc. I just came from World War III, except no one was fighting except my wife. She was having one massive argument with someone. Couldn't have been me— I was calm, solution-oriented, non-judgmental, even made teamwork comments. I didn't argue one point. But she kept going on and on. I couldn't even understand what the problem was in the first place."

"What did she say the problem was?"

"I can't tell. She was a raving lunatic. It started that I don't do anything around the house. But I've been doing a lot around the house lately. I've been home a lot more than ever before, which she admitted, but then she says that because I've been around lately, and being a good husband, it's showed her what she's been missing all these years, and she's pissed because of the way I treated her before I was being good to her like I am now."

"That's a mouthful."

"It gets worse. Then she pointed out that now that I've been simplifying our possessions and my life, she's always the bad guy because she's not as happy as everyone else. I don't understand that 'cause she was into it more than I was, especially with the checkbook and throwing out all the garbage. Finally, she says that I don't seem to care anymore. I was thinking I cared more than ever, but I think she sees my not arguing as a sign that it doesn't matter. It's funny, I get rid of the girlfriend, I look to my home for pleasure, I even start to look differently toward my wife as a lover and friend, and now I don't care. What's going on?"

Time to open the piggy bank. I hope I have something worthwhile inside.

"Seesaw effect. I call it the seesaw effect. Picture the relationship like a playground seesaw. As long as both people are out on the edge, you can bounce up and down. If both people are in the middle you can also bounce."

"But, it's not as exciting a ride on the inside."

"Good point, we'll get back to that. Now, when one of the two people moves toward the middle—toward the fulcrum—the other person has to move also, or the bouncing stops. You were both on the outer edge of the seesaw. You moved toward the middle, which is a steadier, more logical area. She's still out on the seesaw a little. Naturally, she's going to feel like a bad guy when she's on the extreme and you're in the moderate zone."

"Just a balance thing then. How do I get her into the middle, or should I go to the extreme?"

"That's the choice people have to make. You said the outside had a more exciting ride. Excitement can be created by the arguments, the complications, the affairs, those kinds of things. Excitement isn't desirable unless it is positively created. You were quite excited when I first met you."

"So excited I was ready to blow my fricking brains out. Why doesn't she just move into the middle with me, then?"

"Mike, people are a little intimidated by the middle. They sometimes are concerned that the middle lacks emotion, passion, that people in the middle are all the same or as you wife says 'people in the middle don't care.' "

"Why do they think that, Doc?"

"Can't answer 'why' questions, Mike. For some reason, we have become a society of strong opinions, attack or be attacked, win or lose. Everybody has to do everything at once. Moderation is not very popular. People don't realize that moderation is not mediocrity. The middle of the seesaw will become attractive again when people realize it's fun, there's room for everything, and people in the middle can still be different from each other. They don't have to be the same. Mike, I want you to do an exercise for me, I want you to describe your wife."

"Well, she's a good woman, a good mother. She goes to church. She … uh … well, she gets hysterical over little things. She likes to nag a lot. She keeps harping on things until she drives you nuts. She is terrible with money. She likes to spend a lot, although we've cut back recently. She tries to get along with people, but she talks about them a lot. She knows what everyone is doing all the time. She'll get on the phone with her girlfriends and gossip for hours. She can't have a real good time. She always has to ruin it. I think she just can't fully relax. She likes those stupid talk shows, which I think are the most bogus things in the world. And the damn soap operas. She'll even tape them. You know, those shows where someone's always pregnant by the wrong person, and there's always someone dying. She even likes those pain-and-suffering, eat-your-heart-out movies, where someone finds out he or she has a terminal disease in the first five minutes and it takes the rest of the two hours for the person to die."

"I've heard enough, Mike. I guess if she didn't go to church you wouldn't have anything good to say about her."

"Now don't start getting sarcastic on me, Doc."

"Well, you didn't say a lot of positive things. You sure handed out the negatives."

"I know. We covered that. You can't keep criticizing your team-mates and expect to be on a winning team. I guess I need to work on that some more."

"Mike, you didn't identify negative characteristics, you just said them in a negative fashion. For example, I like some talk shows, does that make me a jerk?"

"You like those shows whose guests are transvestites who have vis-ited with Martians in Graceland?"

"That sounds interesting, but I probably wouldn't watch that one. I like the talk shows where they bring on guests who talk about whatever new stuff they are doing. Like that 'Regis and Kathie Lee' show in the morning, or 'The Tonight Show,' 'Late Night,' or 'Good Morning America.' "

"Well, those aren't like all the others. I guess they're all right."

"You have to approve of my likes?"

"No, I didn't mean it that way. (long pause) But, I guess I said it that way. And I guess I thought it that way, so I'm doing the evalua-tion thing again and overcomplicating matters. How do I catch that a little earlier?"

"To start, Mike, let's look at all those aspects of your wife that you pointed out as mere differences from you. You don't want her to be the same person, you want her to be different. She won't join you in the middle of the seesaw unless you let her maintain her differences."

"I would like her to mirror some of my beliefs and likes."

"Mike, you ain't lookin' in the mirror if the reflection isn't you. She's different, all on her own. She doesn't think like you, doesn't feel what you feel, doesn't talk like you, doesn't want the things you want. She doesn't even perceive the color red the same as you. Most fights start when peo-ple fail to recognize their differences. They want their spouse or partner to think the same way they do, reflect the same beliefs. You can't solve the problems in a relationship until you first recognize differences. Now, describe her in language that recognizes differences from you."

"Well, let's see. She likes information shows about people, I like information shows about nature. That's the talk show thing. Pretty good, huh?"

"Amazing, sort of like when the dog you're training sits for the first time."

Mike got the laugh.

"She's tuned in to her emotions and feelings, where I'm more into concrete, right-in-front-of-you matters. She persists on one topic until it is resolved, whereas I'm a little more laid back. She likes watching people's pain and suffering ..."

"Whoa, Mike. Rephrase."

"She likes to watch real-life dramas that involve human suffering, while I prefer adventure films. She also enjoys talking with others about personal information, and I like to keep to myself more."

"She has now become someone you can live with. Whereas before, you made it impossible to survive with her. Remember, recognize the differences between you and her, and you'll be taking the first step toward solving a problem between the two of you."

"OK, with all that said, what the hell do I do about this fight she's having with me? How can I change the past history from last year that she's fighting with me about?"

"Maybe that's not the issue. Remember, your wife is tuned more into feelings; you are more tuned into practical matters. Maybe now she's tuned into her own feelings and that can't be put into practical terms. Maybe she is talking about the past to describe other times she's felt this way. You may have to forget the practical level and just talk about the feelings she's having."

"You mean what we are arguing about, or what she is saying is not *really* what is bothering her? How do I approach her?"

"Let me tell you a story about my parents, my piggy bank, and some marbles. I remember when I was a little kid ..."

EXERCISES

This chapter is the first of three chapters on resolving problems and conflict in relationships. Relationships will be less likely to survive without a technique for the resolution of conflicts. The simpler the technique, the better chance you have for solving problems. This chapter deals with the first step—recognizing that the other person in the relationship is different from you. Each person has different likes and dislikes, different opinions, and even different perceptions of common events. If you can recognize these differences, you can work toward ending an argument before it begins. Remember, do the exercise yourself first, before you look at Mike's answers.

Exercise 1

First, list 15 descriptive sentences about yourself. You can include your likes, personality characteristics, how you make decisions, and so forth. Try to list a couple of your favorites, like your favorite color or favorite food. Leave space under each sentence for a second sentence. If you do these exercises with a partner—a spouse, girlfriend, or boyfriend— have that person make the same list.

Exercise 2

Now, under each sentence write a sentence on the same subject but which describes your partner. For example, you may have listed "likes westerns" for yourself, and now will list "likes dramas" for your spouse. Look at some of these differences. If you have done this together, trade lists.

Exercise 3

Finally, make a list of issues that you and your partner knowingly disagree on. Make this list as complete as you can. Do not put down who chooses which side; just list the issues. Try to include in this list anything you might have argued over in the last few months. Save this list because we will use it later.

MIKE'S LIST

Exercise 1 and Exercise 2
Descriptive sentences about self and partner

I like to hunt
> She likes to shop

I think rationally before I act
> She acts on intuition and emotion

I enjoy sports
> She enjoys drama

I tend to get hurt easily
> She gets hurt easily

I don't express my emotions well
> She is very emotionally expressive

I enjoy excitement
> She likes everything calm

I like to lift weights
> She likes aerobics

I enjoy history
> She likes reading old English books

I obsess a lot
> She obsesses

I throw caution to the wind
> She is methodical

I like to go out and drink
> She prefers to dance

I believe in strong discipline
> She believes in talking everything out with the kids

I believe in a strong family
> She believes in a strong family

I am a night person
> She is a day person

I am often too inflexible
> She is often too inflexible

Exercise 3
Issues in marriage

Child rearing
Sex life
Spending/saving money
Her parents and the boys
Cleanliness of home
Time together
Drinking too much
Fixing up house

SESSION 15

Seeing Life Through a Toilet Seat

I remember when I first lived with a person of the opposite sex (other than my mother), I was accused of purposely creating problems because of my treatment of the toilet seat. I grew up in a house with all males, except for Mom. I had no idea what I was being accused of, but, wanting to please, I would clean the toilet every couple of days, figuring I must just be messier than other men, that must be what she meant. One day, this woman I lived with screamed that she just sat in toilet water and asked (in full volume) why I purposely left the seat up after I was finished going to the bathroom.

Purposely? I thought. It never occurred to me to put the seat down, yet, I was perceived as being disrespectful. I asked other women about this, and found out there was a common concern with toilet seats among females. In fact, I've come to learn that the toilet seat issue has been a battleground for the sexes since indoor plumbing. I didn't realize it then, but I had stumbled on to one of those age-old secrets of life: People—in this case, men and women—are different, and if I wanted to be able to live with others, I had better learn to respect those differences. This is what I call seeing life through the toilet seat.

I started the session by relaying this story to Mike.

". . . So you see, Mike, if we are to live with others, we must try to see life through the toilet seat."

Mike had one of those patient, slightly condescending looks on his face, like when an old person tells you for the thousandth time how he walked five miles to school through the snow.

"Great story, Doc. Toilet seat, huh? I'm going to remember that

145

one. See life through the toilet seat. Now that's advice for the 21st century."

"That's right, Mike. See life through the toilet seat. Remember it, and your relationships will be much better."

"Oh, I'll remember it all right, Doc. I won't be able to *flush* it out of my mind. It's in the *can*, so to speak. It's a real *piss-a.*"

I love it when people have fun in therapy, even if it's at my expense. When it's fun, I know people will remember what we talked about.

". . . without that advice my life would be all *clogged up.*"

"OK, enough, Mike. Time to move on."

"Sorry, Doc. Guess we should just *plunge* forward."

Ever notice how this kind of humor tends to entertain the speakers more than the listeners? As I listened to Mike sculpt his puns, I knew that many of the problems we had faced in his life were settling. He was quick-thinking, enjoyed life, and was self-entertaining. This is a sign that someone has been successful in simplifying his life. Now if I could just get him to be less corny.

"Mike, how did it go with your wife this week?"

"It's strange, Doc. I just sort of kept pointing out differences without my usual negativity and we had some good talks about differences. But we could only get so far. Then it was like, we're different, now what? Then we would start to fight a little over why I should be more like her, or she more like me. The fight would then be cut short because we knew it was futile. Strange, though it seems like we're getting a little closer after all is said and done. We are communicating really well."

"Mike, people battle over differences even if they recognize that it's 'just a difference.' The next step after recognizing differences is to begin a process of respecting what it means to be different."

"Isn't recognizing differences the same as respecting the differences?"

"No. Most relationship battles occur over the simple fact that there are differences and each person tries to impose his or her will or thoughts on the other. Most people don't understand that part of respecting someone or something involves trusting."

"There's that word, trust. I've gotten to the point where I'm not even sure what trust means because it is used so much. Simplify trust for me, oh guru of simplicity."

"You are in the mood today. Trust, in my simple terms, means first believing that another person's primary intention is not designed to do you harm, and secondly, believing that the other person is capable of handling a situation on their own."

"OK, we're going to have to dig into this one. I disagree with you, because I think in every relationship, when a fight breaks out one person will be defensive even if it means causing harm to the other person. In fact, fights often focus on causing harm to another person's argument or story."

"So why do we disagree?" "You said you have to trust that the other person is not intending to cause harm, and I say at some point in every relationship there will be an intent to cause harm. Thus, by your definition, trust can't happen in any relationship. So it's not simple. I rest my case. Touchdown pass at the gun. Three-point shot at the buzzer. I win."

Mike holds up fingers to indicate he was Number One. He was really enjoying himself today. And I have to admit, I was enjoying watching him parade his sense of humor and good feelings about himself.

"Did you watch 20 straight hours of Three Stooges reruns again yesterday? Defending oneself is different from having a primary goal of hurting someone. In self-defense, anything can happen. Hurting someone is a direct intention to attack for the sole purpose of causing pain, not deflecting pain from oneself. Trust means believing that the other person is not going to attack for the sole purpose of causing pain."

"What's the difference if they are defending themselves, thus causing pain or intentionally attacking to cause pain? It hurts just the same."

"Not if you want a simplified relationship. In a simplified relationship where trust is present, you will see an attack as an expression of hurt and respond to the hurt, not the attack. Then, the argument doesn't progress."

"So you're trying to convince me that if my wife is attacking me, and I trust her, then she is really telling me that she is in pain or feeling attacked, and I need to respond to her feeling instead of my desire to fight back. That's a real strange view of life."

"It's like looking at life through a toilet seat."

"I knew you'd work that in somehow."

"Full respect of her differences means trusting her motives, and believing that regardless of what is said or done, she wants things to be better. Respect is giving up the desire to win in a relationship. Simple."

"And what do you mean by believing that the other person can handle the problem?"

"The second part, Mike, is believing that your wife has the solution to the problem, and you should consider her solution first. Sometimes that solution might be to ask advice, sometimes that solution might be to do something you don't want to do. Sometimes the solution may seem totally illogical to you, but you are best to consider it as a means to a solution that your wife has devised and respect it as such."

"What if I know the solution won't work?"

"Trust your wife's desire to try. Let her fail with it."

"This is too heavy. Make it simpler."

"OK, follow close. The first step in a relationship is to recognize that the other person is different than you in thoughts, feelings, even … "

"The way the person sees the color red."

"Right. Second, you must respect the differences by trusting that the other person is acting not primarily to cause you harm, but to solve the problem. This means not attacking back when you feel attacked, not demeaning the other person's solutions to a problem. That's respect. Simple enough."

"Seems simple."

"Then let's test it by learning how to communicate respect. Let me give you a situation: Your wife is upset over the credit card bill you ran up on the family vacation. She attacks you the second you walk in the door after working a double shift. She wants to sell your antique drum set to pay it off. What do you say?"

"Before or after I put my fist through the wall?"

"Was this too hard for starters?"

"It would be a test. OK, so she doesn't intend to hurt me with the drum set thing. Well, normally I would tell her that was the stupidest thing I'd ever heard, that we probably ran up the bill buying stupid tourist crap she likes. We should sell fifty or so pairs of her shoes if we'd sell anything. Then, we'd get into a big fight and not talk to each other for a couple of days."

"And who'd win?"

"No one. But I'd still have my drum set. Let's see ... communicate respect. How about, 'Gee, hon, that is a big bill. I guess we'll have to figure out some way to pay it off, but let's not get hysterical and sell the drums.' I'm not even close, am I?"

"Nope. Toilet seat is pretty much up on that response."

"Go ahead, hit me."

"Let me give you a couple of choices.

1. Honey, I know you're upset, but you don't have to attack me. Give me the bill and I'll take care of it.

2. Calm down! Don't worry about it. It's no big problem. We'll get through this one.

3. Wow! You're really upset. We must have really gone overboard on vacation. You must have been thinking about solutions for this all day."

"Well, the third one's the obvious choice. But what about the drum set? You don't even mention it. That's what she said to get a response."

"If that's true, then what she wanted to say was that she was very, very upset. She was not doing it to cause harm to you, but to get you to understand. She wanted the toilet seat down. If you communicate to her that you know it upset her a lot, you've shown her respect."

"OK, give me another one."

"Your wife believes you were wrong for spanking your child for a day of acting up, cursing in company, and throwing things at cars."

"Man, you are good at examples. This stuff really happens."

"Your choices:

1. Let me do what I decided. This is between my son and me."

"Obviously not, Doc."

"2. Honey, I respect that you disagree, but this is the way I'm going to handle it; you can handle it however you choose."

"Getting warm."

"3. I did what I thought was the best thing at the time, but I recognize that you disagree, and I see you feel very strongly about it. Maybe we could discuss how we both want to handle this kind of thing in the future."

"This isn't so hard. My turn to come up with an answer on my own. Give me one."

"Your lieutenant calls you in and says you completely botched an arrest on a stolen car because you filled the forms out wrong. So he lets the guy go. He tells you that you're a lousy cop. You thought you did it right."

"Another hard one. Let's see. He attacked me because he was emotional. 'Lieutenant, I can see you're very upset by this. You would-n't criticize me so strongly if you were not. I felt I did the best I could at the time.' I remembered that, Doc. 'So, Lieutenant, could you go over the paperwork with me so I can see your toilet seat, I mean, point of view?' How's that, Doc?"

"Three-point shot at the buzzer. Score! You won!"

"Boy, Doc, this session really went *down the drain.*"

"Isn't if funny, Mike, how our time happens to be up just after that last pun."

EXERCISES

The second step in the process of simplifying problem-solving in rela-tionships is to learn to communicate respect for the other person's dif-ferences. Many fights in a relationship are solely over one person feeling he or she is not getting the respect they deserve. In a relationship, there is no such thing as deserving respect—it must be given automatically. You must believe in yourself to give respect automatically. Automatic respect is what it means to be part of a team. Automatic respect is built on that common bond; it is part of 'holding the line.' If you recognize the differences in your relationships, communicating respect will make the final step in solving the problem very easy. The exercises below are to help you communicate respect.

Exercise 1

In the following situations, construct a response similar to the respons-es in the session. Remember, communicate respect.

- A friend calls and is very upset because she is sure you said some-thing about her behind her back. You do not know what she is talk-ing about.
- Your spouse is upset because you were out with your friends when the dishwasher broke and your help was needed.
- Your boss is upset because your were a day late on a deadline for a report, due to a computer failure.

- You get into a no-fault car accident and the man in the other car claims that it was your fault.
- A colleague at work feels you are doing a little too much kissing up to the boss and confronts you about it.
- A friend is very upset that you won't join him on a camping trip because you have responsibilities he does not understand.
- Your daughter wants to quit the basketball team because she feels she is not the best player on the team.
- Your neighbor denies having the ladder that you know you lent him.
- Your spouse wants you to change plans that you made a long time ago to do something else together that day.

Exercise 2

Reread the list of differences you made after the last session. Now pick three or four of them and, over the course of the next week, communicate to the other person that you respect your differences in those particular areas. It might take some ingenuity to figure out how to work statements of respect of those differences into normal conversation. Challenge yourself to work as many respectful statements as you can into the course of a week.

SESSION 16

Giving In, Out, Up, and Your All

You acquire a strange sort of wisdom being a therapist. You live through so many lives in addition to your own. You see the full cycle of a life span many times over, through different people of different ages. You see the problems and the pains. You learn what goes away and what doesn't. You see change, and the human resistance to change. It's been called the third eye, the sixth sense. You feel what is going on with people around you.

At this point in Mike's therapy, he had made tremendous changes: His pain had been replaced with the positive aspects of his character. He simplified and recaptured himself. He had his self-esteem back. He was comfortable with others. He had his sense of humor back. He had made the changes he felt he wanted from therapy.

But, Mike had also made a male friend, perhaps at a deeper level than any in the past. I guess they call it male bonding. He had found a safe person to whom he could express himself and let the previously scary parts of himself come out. He would have trouble leaving that friendship, but he had to. I knew it was time for Mike to leave. He didn't know himself yet. Yep, it's a strange sort of wisdom you get from being a therapist.

A few weeks passed between this session and the last. Mike canceled twice, for a variety of reasons; mostly he just was busy. Therapy was obviously no longer the priority it had been months ago. Mike came into session straight from the gym. He had that pungent, just-worked-out, manly smell I remember from football locker rooms. On his head was the old headband I remember so well from the first few sessions.

"Ah, the headband's back. Haven't seen that in awhile. You all right?"

"Yeah, it's just a headband today. I found it in the drawer with my workout clothes. Figured I'd put it on for my workout. Nothing symbolic today."

(Even as non-analytical as I am, when someone tells me something is not symbolic, I start to think it might be.)

"So, how are you feeling?"

"Really good, Doc. My wife and I are getting along pretty well—in fact, very well. The kids are great. The job has given me some special duties, investigative stuff. Cross your fingers, I might be considered for detective next time. That's usually what it means when you get placed in this group."

"That's really great, Mike. Wow. A lot has happened in the last month."

"Yeah, Doc, I'm sorry about canceling on you those couple of times. I just got busy with the new job and all."

"No problem, Mike, these sessions are for you, not me."

(The patter of the talk is a good indication that he is ready to separate. I used to get a feeling of rejection when separating from a patient. Psychology is one of the few disciplines where you work your way out of a job, work your way out of relationships. After a few years of therapy work, I learned to feel very good about saying good-bye. I learned to think of it as an opportunity. I guess I listened to what I had been saying to my patients for years.)

"Mike, there's something else I want to teach you in the relationship area. I want you to get into an argument with me."

"Doc, I don't want to argue with you today."

"Come on, Mike. Think of something to argue with me about. One last good, old-fashioned brawl. We should have one good argument before we finish this therapy thing."

(I tried to show Mike that I was aware therapy was coming to an end. It would make him relax. Besides, I had an agenda and I wanted to get one last lesson in before he was pushed out of the nest.)

"Okay, Doc. I know what we could argue about. I think all the hype about Notre Dame football is overplayed in the sports history books. The Florida teams, like Miami and Florida State, are obviously the teams that will make college football history in the future."

"Boy, when you pick a topic, you pick a zinger. We're not talking just college football—this is religion to a Notre Dame grad."

"Since you didn't say anything to try to prove me wrong, I guess you agree."

"Far from it, Mike. Notre Dame *is* college football. When they decide who goes to bowl games, Notre Dame is treated like its own conference."

"But that's just because of the hype, and they refuse to join the rest of the college football teams and be in a conference. They believe their own press."

"They don't need a conference. No other team has more national championships, more Heisman Trophy winners."

"That's just because they were around when few other schools were. And because there is this bunch of empty hype the players and the team get extra consideration. The only reason they have all that hype is because they present themselves as a group of renegade Catholics. Like you said it is almost a religion. They build on that to stoke the hype-engine."

(He is pretty good in a fight, or he had thought a lot about this before he brought it up. He probably has wanted to set me straight for awhile and has rehearsed his argument. I'm at an extreme disadvantage on his home court.)

"Mike, you obviously have never seen a live Notre Dame football game in South Bend. There is nothing more exciting in sports. Nothing more exhilarating."

"How can you call a team that hardly ever passes exciting? They just run and run behind a bunch of oversized buffaloes they put on their line. Dull! Look at a Miami or a Florida State game and it's fast action, passes, speed. That's football, not hype. You should be able to go down in the history of college football if you don't have anything to do with the pass."

"A Notre Dame coach invented the forward pass, Mike."

"Really?"

"Yeah, Knute Rockne in the '20s."

"Oh ... well ... sort of shoots my argument."

"OK, Mike. What just happened?"

"I guess you won the argument."

"Is your mind changed?"

"No, I just got trapped in a corner and lost the battle of words. I still believe what I want to believe."

"That's an important distinction, Mike. Winning an argument doesn't mean you have to change someone's mind. It just means you win the battle of words. If there is one winner, usually the feelings stay the same or even get more hurt. The goal of an argument in a relationship should be for both people to feel as if they came out all right, that they both won."

"Let me get this right. You're saying that two opposing sides—two people who are arguing the exact opposite—should each feel they won an argument. Doesn't sound logical, Doc, and certainly doesn't sound simple."

"But it happens that it *is* both logical and simple. The third step to solving problems in a relationship is the resolution stage, the compromise stage. The key to a good resolution is that both people must feel they've accomplished something when the problem is solved. If both people are committed to finding a resolution, then both sides will have won. In all the business books it's called the 'win-win situation.' Make your fights a win-win situation."

"OK, let's say there is a problem. How do you go about making it a win-win situation?"

"Well, the simple principles of giving in, giving out, giving up, and giving your all."

"I'm ready for this. Make it simple."

"Giving in means that both people decide one person should make the decision in a situation. This works best if one person has a stronger attachment to or feeling about the situation. The decision has to be made to let that person *own* the problem. The problem becomes all theirs, no interference. Sometimes letting one person have control may require the other person to take control of some other situation just to maintain balance. Giving in means one of them takes control of the problem at hand while the other gives in."

"Give me an example."

"Let's say you have a problem with your wife's family. You both want to handle the problem, but your wife has much stronger feelings about it than you do. You give in and let her *own* the problem. You're out of it. This means you no longer have any say in the resolution, and cannot criticize her decision since she *owns* it. You've given in."

"How do I win if I give in?"

"The resolution has to be more important than what you give up or else this is not the right way to solve the problem. If you don't fight and no one is angry with the result, then both sides win."

"Simple enough. What's giving out?"

"Giving out means that both sides are going to work toward finding a middle ground, give out and bend their views a little to find a balance."

"A compromise."

"All solutions are a compromise; even when one party gives in they are compromising. Giving out means being flexible and finding middle ground."

"You know, Doc, I think most people are willing to do this. But then when you start arguing over where that middle ground is, the whole process starts all over again. Everybody has a different idea as to where the middle ground is."

"You can logically find middle ground by a simple methodical technique: Take out a sheet of paper and list the similarities of the two sides of the argument. Make sure that when you make this list, neither of you tries to state your case during the discussion. Take, for example, the disciplining of the children. You believe the child should be spanked, your wife believes in a stern reprimand, what are the similarities?"

"Let's see. We both believe an action should be taken. We both believe our reaction should have an impact. We both believe there should be a punishment aspect to the action. Actually, that's a situation that we agree on everything *except* the severity of how we should react, not the direction."

"Most fights in a marriage are disagreements over the severity, not the direction of, a problem or reaction. What's the middle ground?"

"Well, we could agree to talk first, then spank if it happens again. Or, we could take something away from the child as a punishment. I guess when you list the similarities, the middle ground is almost always obvious."

"Many times. Sometimes you can't solve the situation and giving up is the solution. Giving up means you agree to just disagree, no more discussion, no resolution. This is sometimes the best choice when you don't have to act on something together or when no decision can be made."

"Doesn't giving up just make everything build up inside?"

"If you let it go, and don't rehearse the argument, nothing builds up. Giving up means agreeing to not change anything, to stay with your current opinions. Quitting while angry is not the same concept.

Giving up, by my definition, is a resolution, not a failure to resolve. When giving up is seen by both parties as a resolution, there will be no build-up of emotions."

"OK, what was the last one?"

"Giving your all. Regardless of which way you chose to go, both parties must give it their all. Resolution must be synonymous with winning. They are one and the same. Give it your all."

"OK, Doc, let's solve our argument."

"Our argument?"

"The Notre Dame football hype argument."

"OK, Mike, go through the steps."

"Here goes, Doc. First, I believe I'm an intelligent person and you are an intelligent person, opinions withstanding. No one is a jerk, as you say."

"Decent start."

"Then I recognize that we have a different belief. I believe that Notre Dame football is all hype, it's just like any other school. You believe that it's special and belongs in its position as the greatest college football program in the world."

"Recognize. Good."

"I respect your opinion. In your mind, your view is grounded in strong basic beliefs that are not intended to harm me. I also respect that you would like to reach some accord with me on resolving our differences, even if you do argue very passionately against my opinion."

"Recognize, respect. You've got it right so far."

"OK, resolve. Obviously neither of us would give in completely, and we could agree to disagree but that's sort of a wimpy solution on this issue. So, our similarities might be that we both agree Notre Dame has had a long football history, the school engenders faithfulness that perhaps makes attending a game more exciting, and your alma mater has proven its lasting ability to produce quality teams over time. Could we both also agree that there are other teams more exciting to watch from a pure football standpoint and that throughout the eighties there were other programs that were more successful?"

"I assume we could agree to that."

"Then we could say that Notre Dame football is special and gets the hype partially because of its longevity, but there are other programs that are also special during certain time periods that don't get the same hype during those times."

I could only smile at Mike. He had learned simplicity in three very important areas of his life. Mike took his headband off and stuffed it into his pocket. He had a sad look on his face. I knew what was coming and I was a little sad too.

"Doc, do you think maybe we could start meeting a little less frequently?"

"Mike, you might be ready to go out there on your own without me."

"Well, I know you wanted to work on spirituality. I still have that little pyramid you gave me."

"Mike, what I want to work on is not as important. Not everyone wants to talk about spirituality. It's something you have to be ready for. Timing is important to changing in spiritual areas. This may not be your time."

"I am pretty happy now. Hell, Doc, I may be happier now than any time since I was in college. I'm not sure I want to do anything different. I don't want to complicate things by delving deeper. What does spirituality do for the rest of this stuff, anyway?"

"For some people, spirituality makes everything solid. It gets them through the hardest times, gives them a sense of where they are going and a feeling of calm. It gives some people their direction in life. But not everyone wants to deal with spirituality at any given time in their life. I'll fully understand if you want to take a break. Just remember that I'm here if you want to delve into simplifying this area."

"I will miss you, Doc."

Mike left with a handshake that turned into a hug. He pretty much dropped out of sight for a long time. He referred several of his fellow cops and would send hellos through them, a safe way to make contact. I heard that he made detective about five months later. His wife sent me a Christmas card and I even received a birthday card from his family (cops can check motor vehicle records for birthdays). It was nice to get them.

About fourteen months after his last session, I got a call from Mike. After a few minutes of nervous small talk, he asked how he would know when he was ready to simplify his spiritual life. The fact that he was asking meant it was time for him to come in and take a look. We set up an appointment for the next week.

It is my contention as a psychologist that one of the biggest problems in the practice of psychotherapy is that most therapists do not deal with issues of spirituality. The fear is that spirituality removes therapy from the realm of

*scientific practice, that it removes it even further from the tangible.
Spirituality is the base and foundation for many lives, not necessarily religion, but spirituality.*

You may or may not be ready to deal with spiritual issues. I would like you to read on, but if you are not ready, please feel free to review the previous chapters, go on to the prologue, and possibly return to read about spirituality at a time when you are ready. We'll await your return.

SUMMARY OF SIMPLIFYING RELATIONSHIPS
Five Steps:

1. Your self-esteem must be independent of outside events.

2. When in a relationship, establish the values of teamwork, having a common bond, and keeping problems within the relationship.

3. Learn to recognize differences between yourself and other people.

4. Respect differences, and make sure you communicate that respect.

5. Try to find a compromise when there are problems.

SESSION 17

Don't Box with God

I especially enjoy the sessions concerning spirituality because I
learn more and more every time. After each new patient goes
through these exercises with me, I change my view, I evolve. Each person
experiences these sessions differently. Spirituality is an area where the
answers truly lie within the people themselves. One common bond is that the
simpler the concept of spirituality, the better it seems to work for people. But
then, almost every religion mirrors that exact sentiment, not only with regard
to spirituality, but about life in general. The simpler, the better.

Mike came into the session very happy to see an old friend. I could tell
by his voice over the phone that something was wrong. I suspected he might
have been friends with an officer who was killed in the line of duty the week
before. He was decked out in a suit and tie, very dapper. He looked like a
detective from one of those TV movies, except he wore that old headband
around his wrist.

"Very dapper, Mike. Real detective looking."

"Yeah, you've never seen me dressed up. I have to wear a tie to
work now. I'm not sure if the promotion was worth wearing a tie every-
day."

"You look great. Ugly tie, of course—looks like a cop picked it out.
But the rest of the outfit is great."

"Huh, my wife hates this tie too. She picked out the suit. Anyway,
I feel great. Life is pretty good to me. I kept your advice, for the most
part, and it's still simple. I spend a lot of time with my family and I love
it. I just thought I'd come in for a session or two. Been feeling a little
strange lately."

Mike tugged on that headband.

"Did you know Pete?"

"You don't beat around the bush, do you? I almost forgot you were that way. I trained Pete when he came on the job about five years ago. Best rookie I ever worked with, just had a natural instinct for the job. We got real close. I sort of became his big brother. We'd go to lunch maybe once a month or so. Did you hear about how he was killed? He was working in his friend's store on the weekend doing some carpentry. He heard a commotion next door, and being a cop he knew something was wrong. He went to help out and walked in on an armed robbery/hostage thing. They shot him before he even got fully in the door. The sonofabitches ran and got away. He probably saved a couple of lives in that store. He was a hero, a damned hero, but he never knew it."

Mike was able to hold back his tears only by the anger that swept across his face.

"You know, Doc, I'm not supposed to talk about fairness, but why the hell does the newspaper bury his story on page 14 and put a story about a couple of cops beating up some punk across the other side of the country on the front page? Or look at the paper today. The front page story is about a cop who shoots an armed mugger and there's public outcry—against the cop. We can be either heroes on the back pages or criminals on the front pages. What the hell is the use?"

I learned a long time ago that as a psychologist, or as a friend, when a person is soul-searching it is best to keep your mouth shut until asked to speak. I also learned you can't try to feel the pain of someone who is soul searching or you risk missing the idea completely. Never relate someone's pain to something in your past, it doesn't work. This is where most people just miss the boat when it comes to being a good listener. Feel your own emotions in reaction to seeing a person you care about who is in pain. Then you'll be able to relate to them.

"Doc, you spoke once about helping me find myself spiritually. I'm so lost now spiritually; I don't think there's hope. I don't know if I believe in God. If there is a God, how could he let Pete die, and let that scum run free?"

He looked at me as if waiting for a response. Silence was still the best idea until invited.

"I've been in so many situations where I could have been the one to die. Why didn't I die? It seems so arbitrary. Hell, Pete just had a child a few months ago, his whole life was in front of him. He was a hero . . . page 14 . . . the world just doesn't make sense." *Mike looks over again.* "Are you gonna say something? I'll stop whining for a second if you want to say something brilliant."

"I wish I had something brilliant to say. I agree with you, almost across the board. It isn't fair. Pete's a hero. The newspaper *should* cover a story of a hero cop over a story of a cop making a mistake, and many times they do. It seems so arbitrary who dies and who doesn't. And I can see that you are in a lot of pain and have a lot of questions. And I feel bad for you right now."

"Doc, you once told me that something good can come out of these bad things. What good is going to come out of this?"

"I don't know what good will come out of this for Pete's family or for society. I guess that depends on their reactions down the road. I know that a lot of cops who worked with Pete are now reevaluating their lives, because some of them have been calling my office. Some of them will change, that's good. And as for you, I suspect we're going to spend some time working on your spirituality; maybe that could be good, too."

"And what good is going to come out of this for Pete?"

"Pete died in the act of helping other people. Nothing could be nobler. Since I believe in an almighty power, Pete is well taken care of because of his nature. He died in the service of others. I can offer no more than that thought."

"And that's precisely my problem—I don't know if I believe in God."

"Do you believe there is more to life than flesh? Do you believe that every human has a spirit?"

"I don't know."

"Mike, I want you to try an experiment. Put this blindfold over your eyes. I'm going to turn up the air filter so you can't hear any other noises around the room. Now, since you can't see me or hear me, I'm going to leave the room and re-enter three times. I want you to tell me when I am in the room."

We did the experiment and every time I entered the room Mike knew it within 15 seconds. Then we switched, and I was able to tell the same. I've done this numerous times with people and it works for those who are willing to concentrate. It may not work every time, but when it does it's sure more than chance.

"Now, Mike. Why do you think you can do that?"

"I don't know, but it's sort of eerie."

"Mike, when you've been to a funeral home and you're next to a dead person, do you feel something is missing? Can you tell the person's dead?"

"Yeah, always. In fact, I've had two people die on the scene, and I could tell then too. It was like something left their bodies."

Cops report this experience over and over. Death seems to be perceptible.

"So are you saying that's the spirit, Doc?"

"I'm saying there's more to a body than flesh and electrical impulses. There's something we don't yet fully understand."

"I can buy that, but I still am not sure I believe in God."

"Why do you even talk about God if you don't believe? Do you ever do good things hoping God is watching, or avoid bad things being afraid God is watching?"

"Well, I don't fully believe in God, but just in case there is a God I don't want to be caught being too bad. So I sort of half believe, that way I might get some consideration just in case there is a God."

"Consideration after death? What happens after death?"

"Well, I was raised a Catholic, so I guess I used to believe in heaven and hell. I'm not sure about that though. Could be reincarnation or another existence after death. I believe something happens after death."

"So something happens after death. Who controls what happens?"

"Nature, maybe. Which I guess is like saying there's a God, except making it less like it was one entity."

Mike starts laughing.

"Do I sound as stupid to you as I do to myself, Doc?"

"I guess sounding stupid means talking about something we don't know about, and if that's so, we're both stupid in this case. You just aren't as comfortable with sounding stupid."

"Well, I should be, I've had enough practice. You know, I think I believe in the existence of a higher being or a God, or at least some order to things, but I don't believe in the Catholic Church like I did when I was younger. You're a Catholic, Doc, do you believe in the Catholic Church?"

"Yeah, I also believe in the Methodist church and the Baptist church and the Jewish religion and the Buddhists and the Tao and Zen philosophies, and I could go on."

"That sort of makes sense. You know, I lost the church when I realized it had rules against everything like abortion, contraception, premarital sex, women being anything in the church. I didn't believe the same as them. Why do women have to be so limited in the church?"

"I'm not sure Mother Theresa feels real limited."

"There's a good example. She'll never be the pope. She might be a saint one day, but she'll never be the pope. I guess I answered my own question. It would be better to be a saint than the pope."

"She's limited in title, Mike, not in the ability to do good. I guess what you are saying is that religion became very complicated for you—too many guidelines for which you disagree. But spirituality doesn't mean agreeing with all the guidelines of a religion. Most priests I know disagree with at least some of the same areas as you. You eventually set your own guidelines, possibly using the church for direction when needed. There is a book called *If You Meet Buddha on the Road, Kill Him*, which basically means you are your own Buddha, your own guru. Don't let others dictate who you are. Believing in one church or one philosophy does not necessarily mean blind obedience. Being spiritual does not mean lockstep obedience to all the rules that someone else has set, although that may work for some."

"OK, Doc, the Bible says we were born free beings. Yet it seems like in accepting God or some other higher order, we give up our freedom. We have a freedom to choose who we are, but Pete certainly did not choose his fate. So where is this freedom?"

"Mike, as best I can figure it, we have a freedom to do, to act. We do not seem to have a freedom *from* actions or events. Remember when we talked about adversity, and we agreed that our reaction determines the outcome. That's a freedom to act. We can act in evil ways or in positive ways. We do not control the freedom *from* things happening, like death, natural disasters, or even some earthly responsibilities. We can try to control something from happening to us, but our ability is limited. Maybe that is where we have to accept a higher order, when we don't feel that our actions can give us freedom from something."

"You know, Doc, I do have real strong beliefs about the way to act toward others. I do believe in something after death. I do believe that sometimes things happen for a reason. And I believe that when I come across a really good person I can almost sense a strength there that isn't in everyone. But why does something like what happened to Pete happen?"

"Mike, we accept that the sky is blue and that clouds appear at times. We accept the changing of the seasons. We can even accept an earthquake or a hurricane, even though it can cause great damage to the earth. We simply have to accept it. Our questions will do no good. There was a musical once called, 'Your Arms Are Too Short to Box with God.' I perceive the title as meaning that I can't fight with God about what He has created. I just have to accept it. I don't understand why Pete died, but I can't box with God. What makes spirituality simple for me is the realization that I have to accept some things without any understanding or reason. Don't box with God, Mike, don't box with God."

Mike cried. I put my hand on his forearm. He grabbed it with his other hand and held tight. He cried for Pete. He cried for himself and the beliefs he lost during his life. I've heard the expression that sometimes "you need a good cry." I think Mike needed this one. I could see him getting stronger as he cried. I could see him preparing to change.

EXERCISES

Exercises that involve accepting and defining your spirituality are highly intellectual. Write down your answers, since people tend not to think things through when just working in their heads. You'll find Mike's responses to the questions at the end of this chapter.

Exercise 1

In an attempt to clarify how you view God or the higher power in the universe, write down the first thing you think of when you view the following roles in life.

Is God or the higher power:

- A kindly parent?
- A stern parent?
- A teacher?
- A judge?
- A nurturer?
- A lawgiver?
- A manipulator?
- A puppeteer?
- A police officer?
- A product to be sold?
- A spouse?
- A child?
- A business partner?

Exercise 2

If given the opportunity to make the decisions of the higher order or to "play God," what kind of role would you play to the people in your kingdom? How would you perceive people if you were the higher order yourself? What expectations would you have of them?

Exercise 3

Make a list of daily happenings that you do accept in your life without full understanding, for example, why the sky is blue. Which of these are decisions of a higher order and which are decisions of humankind?

Exercise 4

Think back to an event in your life when you were unable to avoid an outcome regardless of your efforts. Was this an act of God that you can accept now? Is it possible that you can prevent this event from happening again? If it was not an act of God or higher order, can you think of an event that might be? What kind of statement would you need to say to yourself that would help convince you that you did not have freedom from this event?

Exercise 5

What expectations does God or the higher order have of your behavior and thoughts? Look back to Exercise 2 after you have made your list.

MIKE'S RESPONSES TO EXERCISES

Exercise 1
What Is the Higher Power to You

List your first thought under each description

A kindly parent—gives without return
A stern parent—punishes the guilty
A teacher—provides opportunities to learn and be more aware
A judge—doesn't judge until the end
A nurturer—lets you develop at your own speed
A lawgiver—commandments, rules to live by
A manipulator—always has temptation available to us
A puppeteer—pulls the strings on natural disasters, can change lives
     at will
A police officer—enforces rules, always sees if you break the rules
A product to be sold—church is always asking for money
A spouse—with you all the time, can share inner most feeling with
A child—innocent, believes in you
A business partner—works with you for success and common goals.

Exercise 2
If I Were the Higher Power

If I were the God or higher power I suspect I'd be very active at first, trying to control everyone's lives to make sure things start out right. I see people as needing direction. Maybe this is what God did. Then, I could see just sitting back and looking at how life is going for people, sort of just watching, not intervening much. Sort of like a parent does with their child. He gives a lot of direction first, then backs off and enjoys when the child becomes an adult.

Exercise 3
What I Accept—Is It of God or Man?

the sky is blue   higher order
crime   manmade

drugs	manmade
wind/weather	higher order
daily conversations	manmade
growth of plants	higher order
the way our bodies work	higher order
banking	manmade
work	manmade

Doc, I'm not sure which is which. I'm a little lost on the decision of what is from a higher order and what is manmade.

Exercise 4
Acceptance

One morning, Dad called and said he didn't feel well. I didn't figure it to be a big thing, so I ignored it and went to work. He didn't tell Mom right away because he didn't want to upset her. Mom called that night and said Dad had a heart attack. I rushed to the hospital. He died the next day. I wasn't sure that I couldn't have prevented it had I taken him to the hospital in the morning when he called. I think now that it was meant to happen. I free myself from the event when I think that phrase, "I did the best I could do at the time." I can't expect to know everything and be everywhere.

Exercise 5
Expectations of A Higher Power

I am not sure that God has any expectations of me. I hope I don't have expectations when my children are adults, except maybe to let me share in their lives. Maybe God only wants to share in my life.

SESSION 18

If You Get It Right, Do It Again

I've had several clients ask me why they should add a spiritual component to their lives. "Doesn't simplifying mean reducing the number of aspects of my life?" "I'm not spiritual now, why should I change?" Many would continue, suggesting that developing spirituality meant analyzing thoughts, and analyzing is not simple. At first, I would give them any of a number of "set" answers such as: "I did not say to rid your life of the food that nourishes you and spirituality is that food," or "any change will require complications first, but the labor and toil will increase simplicity in the future." I would, of course, be very satisfied with my answers. They would not.

When striving for enlightenment in Zen Buddhism, the most common mistake is trying to think your way into it. The Christian Bible suggests that we cannot possibly explain heavenly things with the earthly words. I realized that trying to give answers to these kinds of questions could never be satisfying, since the purpose and path of spirituality cannot be understood by description. I find it best to describe only what I see. People with a simplified spirituality seem to be able to manage change better. They seem to be able to handle crises better. They seem to be better able to control their impulses and be less affected by their environment. They seem to have less problems reaching their goals and less problems when they don't achieve what they want. They seem calmer, they seem happier. There is no way to explain with key phrases. People with simplified spiritual beliefs seem happier.

These sessions on spirituality come at varied time intervals, since thought is needed between sessions. Scheduling is less important. This session occurred about 15 days after the previous session, although Mike had missed an appointment. Mike was in a good mood.

"It's good to see you, Doc."

"You too, Mike."

In the past, Mike always made excuses for missing earlier appointments. It is a relief to know he doesn't feel he has to anymore.

"OK, so let's get right down to it, Doc. I went to church last Sunday for the first time in ages."

"And what was it like?"

"It was just how I remembered it. We sat, we stood, we kneeled, we sat, we stood, and so on, and so on. We recited the same prayers we used to, over and over. I mean, I remember that in catechism class some 30 years ago they did some of the same stuff. There's only about a five-minute piece when they actually say something that has anything new to it. Why is the service the same thing every week?"

"Well, Mike, the rituals of the church are very important to developing the religion. Without the constant repetition, people don't get a sense of being part of the church."

"I don't know if I like that answer. It sounds like a pizza boy in Arkansas delivering to Brooklyn."

"What does *that* mean, Mike?"

"Well, he'd have to go a long way to deliver something that's just going to leave a bad taste in everyone's mouth. All these rituals are the long way and they don't taste too good."

I love his images—they can only come from a mind like his.

"Mike, every group has rituals. They are repetitive acts that build the foundation for community and closeness. In a family, the ritual may be something like the family meal, or a phrase that gets repeated all the time. The foundation of the family is built on these expressions of togetherness."

"But, why the movement all the time? Up and down and up and down. And the same prayers over and over."

"Because this is the way that people join together. It's their common bond."

"Is it like that in all religions?"

"Not just religions, Mike. When you study Zen, you sit and meditate, which is an act of ritual that allows you to gain new insights. When you become a member of a fraternity, you learn certain expressions and phrases. When you became a police officer you learned how to do certain things that perhaps have little purpose, but it's the way it is done in that community. College students cheer for teams in a certain ritualized way in each college; generations create a certain language to talk to each other; friends even have certain patterns that they repeat over and over. Ritual brings people together. It identifies you as part of a group."

"I guess it's like the saying, 'if it slithers and has fangs, it's a snake.' "

"Who'd say that, Mike?"

"My dad used to say it."

"What's it supposed to mean?"

"You can identify people by the way they act."

"Oh, OK. I guess that applies."

"But Doc, why are all the rituals in the church the same ones that used to be around years ago?"

"Mike, I want you to try and experiment with me. Just unscramble some words for me. The first word is K-R-B-A."

Ten seconds later. "Bark."

"Good, Mike. Next, N-W-D-O."

Eight seconds later. "Down."

"Great, Mike. Now, P-M-J-U."

Seven seconds. "Jump."

"Do you notice it is taking less and less time? Do you know why?"

"Yes, I noticed it, I guess it's just practice."

"Let's try a few more. Try, D-L-G-O."

Mike and I did about ten of these until it would take him barely more than a second to come up with the answer.

"What have you figured out that has allowed you to do them so fast, Mike?"

"Well, they are all the same pattern. The first letter is the third letter, second letter is the fourth, third the second, and last is the first."

"Great. Now, what if we did a hundred of these?"

"I guess it would become automatic, Doc."

"Right, and that's what rituals do. By repetition they make things automatic. The longer you do something the more automatic it becomes."

"Like the old saying, 'the horse has to have a long tail to swat flies on his face.'"

"Exactly, the long tail is like the long history needed to develop a ritual. A ritual with a long history will help you solve problems in a variety of situations."

It started getting scary when I began to understand these kind of analogies.

"It sort of makes sense, Doc. When I went to church regularly as a kid, I did feel more a part of a community. When our family stopped the nightly dinners, we started being less of a family. Maybe nightly dinners are one of the problems of today. Families don't do that as much because everyone is so busy."

"That's a really good point, Mike. The busyness of many families today ruins the rituals. Being too busy is also a sign of complication. Rituals are a simple way of strengthening spirituality, just as they are a simple way of strengthening a family. Simpler lives have more ingrained rituals."

"A dog will go to the bathroom in the same spot every time."

"Yeah, and it's funny how we look on a dog's life as a simple life."

"So how do I bring simple rituals into my spirituality other than with church?"

"Well, Sunday in church helps simplicity, and if you don't like one church, go to another. I don't believe any religion has a monopoly on God. Today, as in older days, some families might read a passage from the Bible, say a prayer, or hear a daily fable before dinner. That's a ritual. Reading for five minutes each night—whether it be a religious book or a philosophy book or any type of spiritual book—can become a simple ritual that will strengthen you and your family."

"Basically then, Doc, you're saying any type of repetitive act that has to do with making me think about myself, my belief system, my morals, and so forth, will strengthen my spirituality."

"Quite simply, yes. If you are trying to strengthen a certain muscle to make it stronger or larger, you work it over and over until it begins to build. Repetition builds."

"Repetition is so boring though. I mean, what am I supposed to think about while I'm saying some prayer on Sunday that I've said for the ten thousandth time? Everybody seems to be so into it, and I feel like a heifer in a swimming hole."

"Mike, I wish I had all the answers for you. This one I can't answer. Sometimes I find it useful to consider the words I am saying in light of the week I've just lived. Other people have told me they concentrate on one specific part of the prayer and apply it to their lives. Some people have told me they find meaning when they consider the prayer in light of the lessons of the mass that day. I guess there are any numbers of ways to make that prayer come alive each time, and you'll have to work on one for yourself."

"I can see in myself that I've viewed repetition in the wrong light. I've had the wrong attitude, and have seen repetition as a destructive process rather than a building process. I did reps in the gym so that when I played ball I could make the right play. I do the reps in church or at home so that when I'm faced with a moral play, I can hold true to my beliefs. Maybe if more people did the spiritual reps, they would be more consistent with themselves."

"Another good point, Mike."

"Good moral reason may be masked by unfavorable behavior. A person's spirit will guide response to an action. The buildup of rituals helps make that guidance more automatic."

"You make a lot of sense, Mike. It's like when a pig rolls in the mud ... wait a minute ... what am I doing ... pig in the mud! ... I think our session time is up, Mike."

EXERCISES

Rituals pervade your daily life whether you have been aware of that or not. The following exercises and accompanying worksheet will help you discover the rituals in your life. As always, Mike's worksheet is at the end of the chapter.

Exercise 1

List rituals that your family engaged in when you were a child. Remember, a ritual is something done the same way throughout your life, usually to help bond the family together. Include items like the family dinner, bedtime rituals, special phrases that became like family slogans. Try to list at least five rituals.

Exercise 2

Think about your family now and what kind of rituals you use today to bring the family together. If you are single now, you may wish to use your extended family or even a group of your closest friends. Friends also have rituals, such as meeting at the same place for sporting events, nicknaming, gathering for coffee or shopping trips, and so forth. Sometimes it is hard work to realize the rituals that exist in your life, but if you look hard enough you will soon discover them.

Exercise 3

Take a close look at any group of which you are a member and look at the rituals of that organization. This could be any kind of social club, the place where you work, your profession, your community, or almost any group that gathers somewhat regularly. If you are not a member of any organization, look at a group or community around you. Try to find the origin of each of the rituals, as it will help you understand the development of rituals in your life.

Exercise 4

Finally, make a list of three to five rituals that you would like to begin in your own life. Include one in the area of family or friends, one in the area of community, and one which will aid in deepening your spiritual feelings. Remember, rituals are made of acts that are regularly repeated. When making your list, try to decide whether the ritual will be practiced monthly, weekly, or daily. Remember, the more reps, the stronger the muscle.

MIKE'S EXERCISES

Exercise 1

List rituals that your family engaged in when you were a child.

Family dinner, especially Sunday
Watching Wild Kingdom and Disney on TV on Sundays
Reading at bedtimes
We used to call Dad "Pioneer Pop" because he liked to camp
Saying grace before meals
Popcorn with TV at night
Big band music on Saturdays and Sundays

Exercise 2

What family ritual do you have with your family now, or if single, with your friends or significant other.

Playing catch with the boys evenings that I'm off
Family dinner some evenings
Suzie and I go out for Chinese food once a week

Exercise 3

Take a look at any group you are a member of and list some of the rituals of that organization.

One group is my college football alumni:
We all go to a game once a year for alumni weekend
We have nicknames for each other
We have a set of cheers
Singing the fight song before dinner
We always play a practical joke on one of the coaches
We have special drinking games just for ex-players
We meet at the same bar after the game
We send yearly Christmas cards to each other

Exercise 4

Make a list of three to five new rituals you would like to start.

Call close friends once a week, less-close friends once a month
Barbecue once a year with all police squad
Bring family to church with me once a month
Say grace before meals
Join community clean-up program with family once a year
Pick a family TV show to watch weekly

SESSION 19

Be a Good Little Boy Scout

When I was a Boy Scout, I was taught that the true spirit of scouting meant to "do a good deed daily." The image of a Boy Scout helping an old lady across a street pervaded America until it became an icon of our culture. I don't see that Boy Scout picture as much anymore. Spirituality was so much simpler then.

Once when I stopped to help a woman whose car was stuck in the snow on the roadside, she insisted on giving me money for my assistance. When I refused, she became very insulted insistent, saying she did not want to be indebted to anyone, she wanted to pay her way. I told her I had already received my pay by the good feeling I got by helping someone in trouble. She looked confused. People aren't as used to kindness from others as they have been in the past.

As the nightly news becomes more and more violent, as our daily newspapers resemble tabloids more and more, as fighting continues in countries whose names aren't on maps made ten years ago, we have become a society where it is easy to forget the Boy Scout, the daily good deed. All too often, we don't try to help that person on the roadside. When someone lends a helping hand we suspect that there must be an ulterior motive. When we simplify our spirituality, we learn to better accept not only the bad, but even the good actions of others. When we simplify our spirituality we will look for opportunities to help other people.

It had been about three weeks since Mike's last session. He came in rather relaxed.

"I've been to church a lot since our last meeting."
"Why is that, Mike?"
"I don't know. I just sort of like going and taking it in. Strange, I

have been taking a lot in lately, whether it be in church or outside or even just watching people go through their daily gyrations of life."

"Gyrations of life. That's an interesting way to express day-to-day living."

"I guess. Sometimes people seem like they are rowing a boat in the middle of an ocean. They row one direction for awhile, then the current changes and they row in the other direction. All the time they are just being tossed around, never really moving far from the spot where they started, never enjoying the ocean, sometimes never even seeing the ocean."

"Boy, that is a real pessimistic view of the world, Mike."

"Just an observation. If you sit back the ocean current will move you eventually, but no one sits back. I've just been in a real contemplative mood."

"What are you contemplating most, Mike?"

"Thinking about God, I guess. You know, you read those stories about people who die and follow the light in the tunnel. You read or hear about God appearing to different saints and talking to them. You see people that have a calling from God to do a certain job or task in life. Some people who accomplish these phenomenal things credit God with giving them a hand. Other people credit God with getting them through the bad times. What about us ordinary people? Why doesn't God just come to us? Why doesn't he come to me?"

"Reminds me of a joke."

"I'm pondering one of the greatest questions of human existence, and you have a joke. You're amazing. So go ahead."

"There's this really faithful guy who lives in a town and it's been raining a real long time. The news reports indicate that the river going through the center of town will be breaking through the levee and running over. He hears a knock on the door, and it's a fireman who tells him that he has to evacuate because the river is about to go. The man tells the fireman that he believes God will save him. So the fireman goes away. The water gets higher and higher, and the man has to go upstairs in his house as the first floor floods. He hears a knock on the upstairs window and it's a guy in a boat. The water is all the way to the second floor. The guy in the boat says to him, 'You really should leave, the river is just going to get higher.' The homeowner tells him he loves God, and God will save him. The guy in the boat goes away. Finally, the man has to climb to the roof as his whole house is flooded. The water is still rising. He hears a loud noise and looks up and there's another man in a helicopter who tells him, 'You've got to leave, the water is still rising.' The homeowner tells him he believes in God, and God will save him. As the helicopter goes away, the water rises and the man drowns. He goes to heaven and talks to God. He says to God: "I don't understand, I believed in you and you let me drown." God turns to him and says in a thick Jewish accent, "Vhat more could I do? I sent you a fireman, a boat, and a helicopter."

Mike laughs. Then you could see him start to think.

"You know, Doc, when I was really desperate, right before I came here, I prayed that God would help me. Then I walked in on that suicide call and I sort of gave up on God, figured if there was a God he'd never let me see something so gruesome. Then, I came here. Maybe you're that fireman or boat or helicopter. Maybe when I walk into a family fight and offer to take the abusive husband or boyfriend away, I'm the fireman or boat."

"It feels good to be the man in the helicopter, Mike."

"Only if you realize that's what you are. Only if you allow yourself to be the ... "

Something had struck Mike—stopped him mid-sentence. He filled up with emotion. Not sadness, not happiness, but some kind of emotion. His eyes filled with water. His cheeks raised a little, forming little balls up next to his eyes. He cupped his hands over his face as if massaging the tension away, then rested his hands under his chin.

"Doc, that's why I became a cop. I became a cop to get that feeling of doing God's will, the feeling of helping someone unselfishly. Man, has that changed."

"So maybe you did have a calling and lost it somewhere down the road. How did it change?"

"I don't know. You get like cynical as you get older. It's strange. When you go up to a car that's speeding, and you ask for the papers, you're almost god-like. You have god-like powers. You can let the person go, write him up, even write him up for whatever you want. The court will take your word over his. You are the god of your own little universe."

"So you have to make god-like decisions. Did you make them in godly fashion?"

"At first, maybe. At first, you try to weigh the evidence as a god, but you find that doesn't work. You'll let someone go figuring he learned a lesson and he'll speed away right in front of you. Playing God doesn't work. So you start making decisions on more human thoughts, like whether you think the person's a scum bag because of the way he looks, whether you thinks it's a spoiled rich kid who needs to be brought down to earth, or whether it's a good-looking girl that you want to flirt with a little. The powers are god-like, but the thoughts become pure human."

"I guess it's better to have human powers and godly thoughts, than god-like powers and human thoughts."

"That's for sure. Because if your powers are god-like and your thoughts aren't guided with godliness, it does something to your spirit. You get morally weak."

"So, Mike, you were called to be a police officer to help others unselfishly. When you lost your naivete and saw what the real world was like, you started becoming cynical."

"I realized that most of a cop's job is dealing with very insignificant things. I had this vision of doing great things as a cop, but that's not the day-to-day life. I was a god-like creature all right, but in a very insignificant universe."

"One of my favorite quotes, Mike, is from Mother Theresa: 'We are not all called to do great things, but simple things with great love.' "

There was a very long silence from Mike. He seemed to be evaluating something. There is a difference in someone's face when he or she is evaluating something rather than just not being sure what to say next. He ended his silence with a deep breath.

"I want to find that naive cop again. I want to make sure I don't look like one of those guys rowing the boat on the ocean. You always say simplifying means giving up. Well, I want to give up my cynicism and my hardened, or should I say 'hard-ass' attitudes. Where do I start?"

"I sure wish I had the answers to all the questions you ask, Mike! I guess you should start by doing whatever it was you used to do that made you feel the way you felt back then."

"My son's that way. He's a little Boy Scout, and does his daily good deed. Simple. Of course he's only eight years old. Doc, I'm going to start by being a good little Boy Scout. I'm going to, once every day, find something that I wouldn't normally do, unselfishly and be that helicopter pilot in the joke. I'm going to find one good deed that I wouldn't normally do."

"You know, Mike, people always think that to help their fellow man they have to volunteer to some non-profit charity group. They fear they don't have the time. But, you've hit it on the head. Going out of your way once each day, even for just a few minutes, is still helping your fellow man. Doing a simple thing with great love. Not that charity work isn't also tremendously important, but if you don't have the time, don't give up your sense of helping your fellow man."

"And don't stop just because your job makes you help people. That's the mistake I make as a cop. I would say, I'm tired of helping people, I do it all day. It's not the same, and it doesn't necessarily help the spirit."

Mike made a good point, one I hadn't thought about. In social situations, when people find out you're a psychologist, they have to tell you a mental health story. There were so many times I've thought in my personal life, "I'm not going to listen to anyone else's problems when I'm out socially. That's what I do for a living. Isn't that enough?" Sometimes I both hate and I love therapy work. If you listen hard enough, you'll confront every one of your own negative rationalizations for justifying the way you live.

"Mike, do you see how this all ties into simplicity? You are best able to help others if you are not judging them so negatively. You are best able to help others if you are not worrying about competing against them for the best array of possessions. You are best able to help others if you are not so worried about your past, not obsessed with expectations from them, and are able to handle adversity in your own life. In short, you are best able to help others if you live a simpler life."

"And I guess what you are saying is that if your daily life is based on accepting a higher order, accepting the unexplained, some ritual, and helping by choice when given the chance, your spirituality will be more simple too."

"Sounds pretty good to me."

"So how did all of this start, Doc?"

"With the light at the end of the tunnel. The question was, what does God look like?"

"I guess I know that now."

"You do? I look forward to hearing this one."

"Doc, on this earth, God looks like a fireman, a boat driver, a helicopter pilot, and you ... and me."

EXERCISES

I have never met anyone who can't point to a time when someone has come up and surprised them with some act of unexpected kindness. I would also hope we have all been the giver of a selfless act of kindness to someone else. Given that you feel better whether you are either the recipient or the giver of kindness, it is somewhat amazing that these acts do not occur more often. The exercises that follow focus on both phases of being the receiver of kindness and the giver of kindness. As usual, Mike's responses follow the exercises.

Exercise 1

List five times when you have received help from someone from whom you did not expect help.

Exercise 2

Make a real effort on the next five acts of kindness, regardless of how minor, to be very emphatic in your thanks, at least three times your normal response. For example, if someone helps you catch some paper that blew away in the wind, don't just offer a simple "thank you" or "thanks." Be more emphatic, say "That was so kind of you not to sit back and watch me struggle. You don't know how much I appreciate your help, thank you very much." Begin the habit of making eye contact when you make your statement. Try to make this a habit. Too many people pass off a "thank you" without eye contact, and it's much less meaningful. Simple emphasis will make a big difference, and you may be surprised at how much it lifts your own spirit.

Exercise 3

List five times when you have been the giver of an act of selfless kindness to a person when it was not expected of you. Think back to how emphatically the person responded to you. Did the more emphatic responses feel different?

Exercise 4

Begin a list of daily deeds that you plan to do for other people, and try to follow it faithfully for at least one month. People are often surprised to look back at such a list and realize how many lives they have impacted. After one year of daily deeds, you will have impacted the lives of 365 people; that's over a thousand in three years, and close to twenty thousand in a lifetime. By reviewing your list of good deeds, your spirit will gain strength in times of duress.

MIKE'S RESPONSES TO EXERCISES

Exercise 1
Recipient of a Good Deed

Friends picked up kids at Little League when car broke down, even though their kids weren't playing
Teacher took kids home after school and baby-sat on a day when my wife was held up at work
My shrink brought me a college t-shirt when he went to his alma mater's football game
Partner's wife brought over food for me and the boys when Suzie was out of town
Neighbor set up my home computer for me when I didn't know how to do it

Exercise 3
Five Times When I Did a Good Deed

Volunteered to coach in the Police Athletic League when a coach needed a temporary replacement while his wife had a baby
Helped friend do plumbing in his new bathroom
When I got a new snowblower I cleaned out everyone's driveway in the neighborhood
Got my son's teacher a pair of theater tickets for watching the kids
Gave children a ride in squad car

Exercise 4
List of Good Deeds—Two Weeks

Gave friend a ride to airport
Bought CD for wife unexpectedly
Brought partner lunch from home leftovers
Picked up wounded dog and brought to local animal hospital, then back to family
Picked up neighbor's mail while he was away
Stopped to jump start a stranger's car in the grocery store parking lot
Bought a reflector for a neighborhood kid's bike
Helped an older woman down the block replace a glass window that had broken
Helped a friend go for counseling when he was desperate about his divorce
While off duty, I intervened when a counter clerk was being hassled by a mentally ill person. I directed her to a couple on-duty officers
Carried bags for woman to her car
Brought a friend to church with me
Made a phone call for somebody who was afraid to confront a creditor
Went out of my way to tell a person they had left their car lights on

SESSION 20

Just a Pimple on the Arse of a Giant

*P*erhaps *the profession of psychotherapy began in its most primitive form when men first started to communicate with each other. I suppose that one caveman talked about his fear of hunting to another, or one cavewoman confided to the other that she enjoyed the company of one special caveman. Perhaps early man and woman first envied one person's fire-starting ability, or sought to have as good a weapon, fur, or wheel as someone else in the cave. Advice probably consisted of clubbing someone to get something, or make a point. Establishing communication was the key, and this still remains the key for talk-oriented therapies.*

A scene where the therapist in a chair and patient on the couch are talking almost non-stop is a popular image of the therapeutic session. A lot of patients will do just that if allowed, particularly in the earlier sessions. Letting someone do a monologue with minimal therapist input does feel very natural at first, and increasing the dialogue is much easier after people have gotten to know each other. But what feels natural doesn't make that much sense to me. It never made sense to me for someone to hire a professional to sit there and just listen, particularly in the first sessions. If a patient is able to figure out the twists and turns of life, they probably wouldn't need to be a patient. As therapy progresses, he does get better at figuring out what works for him. That is the best time to let him talk, when he has learned and developed a healthier philosophy of life. Then it's time for the therapist to sit back and learn.

Mike came in about three weeks after his last one. He had checked in between sessions, just to let me know he was doing well. He was poised for a deep intellectual discussion. This was a time for Mike to do most of the talking.

"You know, Doc, we're just pimples on the arse of a giant."

(Well, intelligence can be coined in many different ways. I knew if I responded intelligently, he would come around.)

"Even a pimple can leave a mark. Think of how annoying a big pimple back there could be."

"Think about it, Doc. We live here less than a century—just a moment in time considering the history of the world. We occupy the smallest amount of space in our world, much less the universe. We are so insignificant, yet we don't even respect the whole order of the universe."

"Mike, I guess we're like a pimple because we stay for a short time, then we dry up. But while we're here we just make it uncomfortable for the giant ... "

"Let's leave the pimple analogy, Doc. It was supposed to be just an expression, said and left."

"OK, Mike, but I'd never been called a pimple before. I was getting into it. I'll leave it alone, if you just lighten up a little."

(I thought I'd make a demand. Actually, I was just in a silly mode. Psychologists get that way sometimes during sessions. We start noticing strange things about our patients, like a mole hair on a neck or the way a patient's left ear wiggles when he pronounces a certain consonant combination. The worst is when there is a fly in the room and your patient is trying to relate a serious story, but has trouble because the fly keeps landing on him. You got to keep a straight face.)

"OK, I'll lighten up. Well, I've been doing my good deeds. Actually, I've been looking for opportunities to be nice and helpful to people. It's been really rewarding—I feel like I'm doing something, and it feels good. It's also funny how other people start acting toward you when you're always doing good things. My wife and kids have been seeing some of these deeds, and they've changed toward me; they're a little more respectful, positive. That's it—more positive. Other people start getting more positive, too, just 'cause I'm around. People are more caring, and that's made me more outgoing. Who would have thought that these little efforts would have such a huge impact on my life?"

(I just love the inconsistency of people. A moment ago he was insignificant, and now he's making a huge impact. It reminded me of a joke, but I had the feeling this wasn't the right time. I hate when you have to hold in a joke. It's like when you didn't go to the bathroom after your father asked you to before you got in the car, and then having to hold it in across the entire Ohio turnpike.)

"Doc, you have this I-want-to-say-something look on your face. You're probably wondering how I went from a pimple to doing something significant. I think the more you do little things in this world the more you notice how much could be done. You see how everyone else, if they had the right attitude, could do so much more. That's probably why people who go through a program like Alcoholics Anonymous always want to convert everyone else."

I hate when someone reads me like that. I'm supposed to be the one with the "read-people" powers. He's treading on my turf.

"There is a beauty and simplicity in the way the world works. It is somewhat ordered. The rules of science are like the rules of nature. One of my favorites is the pendulum. It swings one way, then goes the other, always picking up more speed in the middle than at the ends. That's sort of like what you have said about the seesaw—it's better if you are in the middle. Simplicity moves you toward the middle and you pick up speed as long as you can control the swings to the ends. Doc, it reminds me of a joke about this guy named Charley who drives a truck ..."

(He started telling my joke. I can't believe he started telling my joke. I wanted to kill him—that was my joke. Now I have to laugh like it was fresh and new.)

"Ha, ha. Good joke, Mike. You really seem to be putting a lot of things together. Just make sure all this thinking isn't getting to you, you don't want to start analyzing."

"I'm not analyzing. I'm observing. I know if I start analyzing I'll start getting depressed or angry. I already thought of that, believe it or not."

"I believe it, Mike. You've thought about a lot of things without me lately."

"I was helping my son the other night with his science homework, and there was this principle called entropy. It says that without work, things get to a random state. I thought how true that was about human nature. If we don't work to keep our minds and bodies in shape, they become random, disorganized. If I don't put some work into my house, it becomes disorganized. Entropy is a law of nature, not just science."

(I was along for the ride this session. Mike is on his way; I'm really not needed anymore. What he is discussing is making him more and more spiritual. I remember when my family would go on a car vacation when I was younger. To keep myself interested, I would pretend I was steering the car with the swiveling knob on the back door window crank. At this point, I almost have to keep up a similar pretense to stay involved in Mike's therapy.)

"How about the scientific principle of inertia, Mike?"
"I already thought about that one."

I knew he had.

"Inertia makes a lot of sense when applied to human situations, too, Doc. When you're going in a direction it is easier to stay moving in that direction. It also takes a jolt to put a mind at rest. It's inertia, pure and simple. That's what happened to me with therapy—I needed that strong initial push. I needed to see that suicide to set me in motion. If people can understand inertia, they could better control themselves. It's simple."
"There's that word again, Mike."
"There's even a scientific principle of simplicity, Doc."

(Parsimony. He's even already thought about all my biggies. He doesn't remember that we talked about this before in Session 9.)

"It's called parsimony. Basically it means always describing something in its simplest terms, accepting the simplest solution first. Sounds like what you try to do with me, make me accept the simplest. It's natural—which brings me to another point I thought about. You know, we always view and talk about nature as if it's something separate from us. We call it Mother Nature. We look to ourselves as a species that destroys nature. But Doc, we *are* nature. We are part of it, and when we do something to nature we are doing it to ourselves. We are really one with nature. I never knew what that meant before, but it makes a lot of sense."
"Mike, that is one of the points that many spiritual disciplines have come upon. The Chinese Tao is based on the concept of oneness. Oneness with others, oneness with nature. Native Americans base their beliefs on the concept of oneness. We have seemed to have lost

that in our culture today because we are too busy drawing lines of separation. This is natural, this is human. We even coin the phrase 'human nature,' as if our nature was run by different laws. It's not."

"I guess by the process of helping others you become aware of the oneness, instead of the difference. Drawing lines of separation is complicating. Perhaps that's why when you stop looking to things to give you status or pleasure, you are simplifying. Having things for status reasons separates you. When you spend all your time evaluating others, or analyzing yourself, you are separating yourself from the world. That's why it's complicating, because you lose the oneness. And when your relationships are built on broken self-esteem, winning arguments, and exercising power, you are focusing too much on problems and making yourself separate from your spouse, losing the oneness. Recognizing that your spouse is different is not the same as being separate from her. Let the differences fulfill your own oneness. A lot of this whole experience just seems to make more sense than before. It's funny, I was happy living simpler, but simplifying my spirituality made me understand why I was happier."

"Mike, spirituality makes everything stronger. That's why people call it a foundation."

"Doc, if it's a foundation, why did you put it at the top of your pyramid instead of at the bottom?"

(Now he did it! I never thought of that, but he's right. I didn't have the answer for the question. Ten years of teaching simplicity and he has to ask that question. I had no answer for him. As all good therapists, I did, however, have a way of dealing with this situation.)

"Why do you think, Mike?"

"I don't know."

"Think about it, Mike. It will come to you."

"Well, I guess when a person's life is very complicated, he has to start at the lowest level, which is to simplify things. A complicated life gets built on things, so it is necessarily on the bottom. The pyramid you showed me was one of change, so it belonged to the complicated life. Once a person simplifies, the pyramid does a complete flip and spirituality is at the base. Relationships are built on the spirituality, thoughts after, and possessions become much less important in the simple life, so they form the small part at the top. After all, the Chinese and Indians you talked about weren't oriented toward possessions at all. So, I guess, the change or complicated pyramid has possessions at the bottom, but the healthier, simple man's pyramid has spirituality at the bottom. Am I even a little close to what you meant?"

There was a little admiration as I looked at Mike. He had come full course.

"Very close, Mike. Very close."

EXERCISES

Since these will be the last exercises in the book, we will focus on tying together all we've discussed. Simplifying your life is a unifying philosophy, and here you'll need to unify a lot of material as you work on these exercises. So this is probably the best time to review all the work you have done. Remember, repetition makes the principles stronger.

Exercise 1

Below are simple definitions of the scientific and philosophical concepts that we have discussed in this chapter. Go through each of the concepts and try to find examples first in Mike's life, then in your own life.

Inertia: The principle that a body in motion will stay in motion unless force is applied, and conversely, a body at rest will stay at rest unless force is applied.

Parsimony: Accepting the simplest explanation or solution to a situation first.

Entropy: Without work or force applied, things will reach a random or disorganized state.

Oneness: All earthly living things come from the same energy source, and consequently are more similar than different. Thus, everything on earth is subject to the same rules and principles.

Try to think of another principle that guides life and apply it to both Mike and yourself.

Exercise 2

Go back to the commitments to yourself that you completed in Chapter 11. Read through what has been written down and add more statements that will help you develop a simple spirituality.

Exercise 3

Go back to the wish list you developed in Chapter 6. Add anything that may have surfaced since you first started reading this book. Also, put a check beside any item on your wish list that you may have achieved since you made the list. Make it a habit to review the wish list and the personal commitment statements on a regular basis.

Exercise 4

Go through the chapter summaries and make sure you understand all that has been suggested to you to simplify your life. If there is something on the summary that you do not understand, review the chapter that pertains to that item. It is important that you not only do the task, but that you understand the reasoning behind the steps you are taking.

Exercise 5

Finally, spend some quiet time in the next few weeks observing the world around you. Take note of simple patterns in life that are repeated across species so that you can begin to see the human race as part of the overall nature of the world. Observe the limits and freedoms of a couple of different forms of life—trees, plants, animals, or people. In these ways, you will begin to feel the oneness around you.

SESSION 21

Not a Wolf in Lamb's Clothes

*T*ermination is one of the hardest parts of the therapeutic process, at least for me. You have to time it right so the patient doesn't become too dependent on you. You have to time it right so there will not be a complete relapse. You have to time it right so that you are emotionally ready to say good-bye. Some psychologists do get attached to their patients.

Mike called about two weeks after his last session. We had a long discussion on the phone about when therapy might end. Together we agreed to have one more review session, one more time where he might feel the comfort of his therapy session. We made the appointment for ten days later. I believe he just wanted to prepare himself. When the time came for the appointment I had one of those both-sad-and-happy-at-the-same-time feelings. I was going to miss Mike. We had laughed together, cried together, and felt the warmth of friendship. But like so many others, it was time to end.

Right before Mike came in I had gotten a call on my emergency line to get in touch with the local precinct immediately. I called the precinct and was told that a vehicle with my plates had been used in the commission of a crime a half hour ago. They asked if I was aware of the whereabouts of my vehicle. I walk out to the parking lot to check my truck only to find everything in order. I came back in, and Mike was sitting in my office laughing.

"Guess it's your turn to play with my head, Mike."

"You see something that looks like a basketball, you've got to dribble it a little."

"Geez, you remember that line."

"How could I forget that, Doc? I go to this guy for help and he's telling me he's going to dribble my head. That's why I stayed around so long. Just to get you back."

"Oh no, I'm really sorry, Mike."

"Sorry about what?"

"Well, I worked so hard at getting you to simplify your life, I've made you into a simpleton."

"That wasn't too good—you're slowing up, Doc. Anyway, so this is it. We've come a long way."

"You sure have, Mike. Do you realize how far? Would you like to see the notes I wrote on our first session?"

"I'd love that. I always wondered what you wrote after I left."

I gave Mike the notes. He went from a real happy look to a real serious look, then he went through a bout of crying a little. He didn't hold back his tears like he used to do. He didn't even look self-conscious. He was real comfortable being how he was at that moment.

"Wow, you captured me a little too well in these notes. I was a desperate man, then."

"Your spirit was awfully weak then, Mike."

"I don't ever want to go back to that, even a little."

"Then don't do anything that will weaken your spirit."

"How so, Doc?"

"When we do even a little thing that is against the way we want to be, we weaken the spirit a little. Each little thing weakens it more and more. As the spirit gets weaker, it becomes easier and easier for us to go against it. Finally, we end up changing who we are. We end up without the same spirit."

"So you mean that when you lie or evaluate someone, you are going against your own spirit. You start to become a different person, even though you still believe in the same things, you change for the worse."

"Yes, that's what I mean, Mike. If you want to be a certain way, don't act any other way. Don't be a wolf in lamb's clothing."

"You know, I see that all the time. I'll arrest a kid and his mom will keep saying he has a good heart. The kid will act real nice, say all the right things, but just makes bad decisions. Maybe what has really happened is that he has weakened his good spirit with bad actions, actions against himself. You can have a good spirit that is weak and you will end up not being a mentally healthy person."

"So the way you avoid slipping back is to keep the spirit strong."

"It's funny, Doc. There are a lot of good spirits who act in bad ways toward each other. Most of the time cops only see the bad parts of life. You usually don't get wrapped up with the police unless you are either a victim or, more likely, a criminal. There's a lot of opportunity to weaken the spirit when you deal with the bad element of society. There's a strong temptation to break the rules when everyone you deal with is breaking the rules and sometimes gaining advantage over decent people. So you get a little rough or treat them with disrespect. Being a cop is a real test of the spirit."

"It's not just cops. Do you think it is different in business? Cheaters sometimes do get ahead, at least temporarily. People who take unfair advantage in business also get ahead, temporarily. It's hard to be honest to a person you know is taking advantage of your weakened position in the business world. Yet, the minute you respond by cheating a person who is taking advantage of you, your own spirit is weakened. No one can damage our spirit like we can."

"I guess with matters of spirituality you have to find something that makes sense both intellectually and emotionally. Each of us is different. Keeping the spirit makes sense in both ways."

"Intellectually and emotionally, I like that. So, how do you combine the two?"

"I still read my personal statement every couple of days, and my wish list every couple of weeks. I've added to them since we've discussed spirituality. They keep me centered."

"That's great, Mike. What did you add about spirituality?"

"I will accept that I do not know God's plan. I will involve myself in a daily ritual to try to learn more about myself spiritually. I will attempt to do one unselfish act toward someone every day. I will always remember that I am one with all that is around me. And, after today, I will avoid acting in a way to weaken my spirit. Those five things will form the basis of my simple spirituality."

I started to laugh.

"Why are you laughing, Doc?"

"Because you didn't ask my approval, Mike. You used to ask my approval for everything. You stated it all so solidly and confidently. And right now, my friend, you can say it better than I can. In the path of a person's life, sometimes you get distracted. As a psychologist, I teach others things and I don't always apply what I say completely to my own life. Right now, I've allowed a little complication to come my way, not a lot, but a little. It's testing my spirit. Working with you has helped me realize that I need to do a little work on myself, to get back to where I was. You may find yourself in this mind-set one day, and remember that, if you always go back to finding simplicity in your life, you can regain the strength of your spirit."

"Funny, Doc. I have fooled myself into believing I knew you, but I really know very little about you. You don't talk about yourself much."

"That wasn't the purpose of our getting together."

"No, I guess it wasn't, Doc. You've been important in my life."

"And you in mine, Mike."

"Don't forget about me, Doc. Hey, maybe one day you'll write a book and put me in there."

"Could be, Mike. Could be."

"Doc, I brought you a little good-bye gift."

Mike handed me a little five-inch square, gift-wrapped box with a huge bow on it.

"This is so nice. Should I open it now?"

"No, Doc, not now."

"When should I open it? It's not ticking at least."

"Doc, I want you to open it at a very special time. Put it on your desk until then."

"When is this special time, Mike?"

"You'll know, Doc. Trust me, you'll know."

I put the gift in my desk drawer. We exchanged our good-bye hugs, and Mike was gone. I knew our association would be left to Christmas cards, announcements, and eventually a retirement party. It's best that way, best for both of us.

About three months after Mike left I was having a horrendous day. The day began when my car didn't start. I'd left the inside light on. When I finally got to the office, I was welcomed with a subpoena to testify in a case of someone I saw one time six years ago before her marriage fell apart. I only remember that both she and her husband were pretty irrational. Then my secretary had double-scheduled a session and, on top of that, I had a cop involved in a shooting and I had to respond. I was going in ten different directions. I opened my desk and saw the small, finely wrapped box from Mike. I thought perhaps it was time.

I opened the box to find inside was Mike's headband. And in a black magic marker he had written the words:

"Keep It Simple"

EPILOGUE

The Moment of Truth

It is traditional in the book industry to include a short list of what people who endorse the philosophy of a book have said about it. Perhaps you might wish to see a listing of people who endorse the philosophy of keeping it simple. Over the history of man, the greatest thinkers in the world have come to the understanding of the importance of simplicity.

"Life is not complex. We are complex. Life is simple and the simple thing is the right thing."
—OSCAR WILDE

"Every man believes he has greater possibilities. Nothing is more simple than greatness; indeed, to be simple is to be great."
—RALPH WALDO EMERSON

"Before we can adorn our houses with beautiful objects, the walls must be stripped, and our lives must be stripped, and beautiful housekeeping and beautiful living be laid for a foundation."
—HENRY DAVID THOREAU

"Rich men feel misfortunes that fly over the heads of poor men. Riches enlarge rather than satisfy appetites."
—THOMAS FULLER, M.D.

"The larger the roof, the more snow it collects."
—PERSIAN PROVERB

"Less is more."
—ROBERT BROWNING

"Only our characters are steadfast, not our gold."
—EURIPEDES

"When a thought is too weak to be expressed simply, it should be rejected."
—VAUVENARGUES

"The greatest truths are simplified. So are the greatest men."
—JULIUS CHARLES HARE AND AUGUSTUS WILLIAM HARE

"The ability to simplify means to eliminate the unnecessary, so the necessary can speak."
—HANS HAUFFMAN

"Teach us delight in simple things. And mirth will have no better springs."
—RUDYARD KIPLING

"Nothing will content he who is not content with a little."
—GREEK PROVERB

"Beauty of style and harmony, and grace and good rhythm depend on simplicity."
—PLATO

"Simplicity, simplicity, simplicity! Say let your affairs be as two or three and not a hundred or a thousand; instead of a million count half a dozen and keep your accounts on a thumbnail."
—HENRY DAVID THOREAU

"Ask yourself if you are happy and you cease to be so."
—JOHN STUART MILL

"We should consider every day lost in which we have not danced once."
—NIETZSCHE

"He must go backwards who would most advance."
—DANTE

"Reduce the complexities of life by eliminating the needless wants of life, and the labors of life will reduce themselves."
—EDWIN TEALE

"Not the owner of many possessions will you be right to call happy: he more rightly deserves the name of happy who knows how to use God's gifts wisely and to put up with rough poverty."
—HORACE

High thinking is inconsistent with high material life based on high speed ...
—MOHANDAS K. GANDHI

"He is a wise man who does not grieve for the things which he has not, but rejoices for those which he has."
—EPICTETUS

"If thou art rich, thou'rt poor; For, like an ass whose back with ingots bows, thou bear'st thy heavy riches."
—WILLIAM SHAKESPEARE

Simplicity! As you can see, it is not a new concept. I do not profess to be a genius who has discovered something original. One psychologist after hearing my presentation told me that I was just presenting what elderly people who have grown wise with age have been saying for years—a simpler life is a happier life. Simplicity follows through possessions, thoughts, relationships, and spirituality. I stand guilty of stealing the ideas of the great thinkers. I stand guilty of stealing the ideas of the wiser elderly. And I have done so for a reason.

With this philosophy, there is an organized system for you to simplify your life, not just a notion or an idea. This is a way for you to interact with psychotherapy without having to identify yourself with some pseudo-scientific or contrived label that enslaves you to a cult-like group that has a hold on your mental health. This is a self-help book that includes spirituality as a part of mental health. And, finally, with this philosophy you will understand why these great thinkers have come to the same conclusion: simple is better, healthier, smarter.

Now it's your turn. Only you can decide. But before you do, one more exercise. I call it "the moment of truth." I want you to picture that you have been told you have just one month left in your life. How will you spend that month? Will you try to gain all the possessions you can before you die, like the bumper sticker that reads, "He who finishes with the most toys wins"? Will you try to analyze every minute left in your life and mourn over all of your lost opportunities? Will you want to be around strangers or spend time with the people you are closest to? Will you want the expensive sports car or the boat to comfort you on your death bed, or would you rather be with the people you love? Will you try to make peace with a higher power, or simply curse God for not letting you live forever? If there were a "moment of truth" in your life, would you choose to live simply and value the simple things?

I've known many people who, in their last days, have spent time with many people just before open heart surgery where the outcome was unsure. I've heard many more stories from others whose time was short. I know their answers to these questions at their "moment of truth." It's your choice. Let now be *your* moment of truth. May your spirit be your guide to the best decision for you.

IS YOUR COMPANY SUFFERING FROM COMPLICATIONS?

15 SIGNS YOUR EMPLOYEE'S LIVES ARE TOO COMPLICATED

- √ Employees are always complaining about something or someone
- √ Work habits have become very inconsistent
- √ Employees look stressed out, going in ten different directions
- √ Cynicism seems to be the primary attitude on the job
- √ Paperwork is way behind, and there are a lot of excuses
- √ The work environment is getting cluttered
- √ Employees are spending too much time spreading rumors and worrying about other people's business
- √ Personal desires are being put ahead of company needs
- √ You keep hearing about your employees having family and marital problems
- √ Employees are not doing what they are told, and are not respecting managers

- √ Employees are calling in sick too much
- √ Productivity is down, Procrastination is up
- √ Everyone is always "passing the buck"
- √ Morale is low, work is "just a job"
- √ Employees are taking their work problems home, and their home problems to work

DR. GARY AUMILLER, *author of the best selling book*
Keeping It Simple, *can bring the wonderful benefits of simplicity to your busine.
agency, hospital, church or community group. His seminars are interesting,
entertaining and informative.*
If interested:

CALL (516) 724-5522